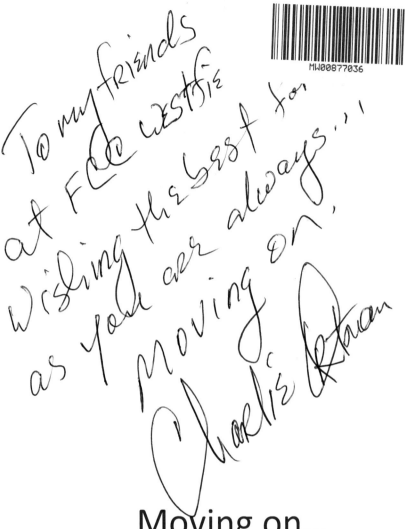

To my friends
at FCC Westie
Wishing the best for
you are always...
as you are Moving on,

Charlie Ortman

Moving on...
Lessons from the Road

by
Charles Blustein Ortman

ISBN-10: 1479221139
ISBN-13: 978-1479221134

DEDICATION

This book is dedicated to those who agree that what we do with the short time we have on this planet matters greatly, and who find that paying attention avails us of some in-credible opportunities, well worth redeeming.

Prologue...

Sometimes things fall into place, and sometimes very nicely...

A couple of years ago I began to think about what I might do with some upcoming sabbatical time. At the time, I had served as Senior Minister of the Unitarian Universalist Congregation at Montclair, in New Jersey, for 14 years and I was ready for a bit of R&R, reflection and renewal. I suspect my congregation was ready for it too, although they would have been too polite to say so. In all honesty, I live a life of considerable privilege and so there were very few limitations on what I might be able to do on my leave. I could travel, take university courses, enroll in special seminars or take part in spiritual symposiums. The only boundary was that I had to do whatever I was going to do within a period of about two months.

I've never been much good at traditional approaches to things, and so a conventional study leave didn't have a great deal of appeal. The interval was scheduled to take place the year before I would turn 60. I know that supposedly you're only as young or as old as you feel, but still – 60 is a major milestone along the road of life. I wanted to do something special, interesting, challenging, satisfying, and maybe even a bit romantic.

I've always been a traveler and love to be in new places and meet new people. And, at least for significant periods of my adult life, I've been a bicyclist, though never on any particularly serious level and certainly not in any competitive way. Still, I love bicycling and I love to travel. The idea of riding my bike across the country occurred to me one day as I rode along the R&D Canal Trail along the Delaware River on the New Jersey and Pennsylvania border. It was a thought that immediately grabbed me. A member of my congregation, considerably my senior, had done it. A colleague of mine, very much my contemporary, had done it. "I'll bet," I thought, "I'll bet I could do that too!"

In my original fantasy of the journey I would set out on my own, braving the elements, stretching my physical limits and relishing in the solitude. My wife, Judy, wasn't thrilled with that idea, neither were some close friends and some members of my congregation. Lions and tigers and bears, and those sorts of things, must have been visions that danced in their heads when they had images of me on the road, I suppose. Their objections began to make sense though, and having some company along the way started to seem like it might be a good idea. I put out some feelers.

A couple of friends, Bill Slezak and Kriss Wells, expressed an interest in joining me on the journey. Bill is a longtime friend from West Orange, New Jersey. Our families have been close since we moved here 14 years ago. Kriss was someone I didn't know quite as well. He was part of a larger group of friends we knew back many years before when we lived in Iowa, prior to my entering the ministry. In the end, Bill and Kriss were my companions on what would be for all of us an adventure of a lifetime. Coincidentally, we were all very close in proximity to our 60th birthdays. But I would be quick to point out that they are both far superior athletes than I will ever be.

I am always looking for opportunities to discover or make wider connections, wherever they might arise. It occurred to me that this ride might provide a great opportunity to do something worthwhile on behalf of a larger cause. I had long been aware of and a supporter of Toni's Kitchen, a superb soup kitchen at St. Luke's Episcopal Church, a neighboring congregation. The slogan at Toni's is, "More than just soup," and it really is. If you were to stop in at lunchtime, you could see the guests and the volunteers all joining together as one community gathered around what is always an elegant, hearty and enjoyable meal.

Along with Sabine von Aulock, a prized member of my congregation who created the campaign, and Mary Ann Renn, Executive Director of Toni's Kitchen, we put together a team to help solicit sponsorships. People could pledge so much per mile, so much per state or whatever they wanted to the ride in support of TK's. Word went out through my congregation, through the local YMCA where I am an active member, and through the wider community that the minister of the Unitarian Universalist Congregation was riding his bike across the country to support a program at St. Luke's Episcopal Church. It was a little like Macy's promoting Gimbel's in *Miracle on 34th Street* and it became quite a bridge-building venture.

The tie in with such a project would be just the thing to make the whole bike trip feasible, a win/win/win! I would take a coast-to-coast bicycle trip, a big plus for me. This service aspect of the trip was an additional plus for me because now I had no good reason to feel guilty about engaging in such an undertaking. And more, it would help to fill a need in our community, which would be a plus for some fairly well-strapped folks who could use the support, to the volunteers who serve those folks, and to members of my congregation who always love to see their minister making a difference in the community.

As it turned out, there was an amazing outpouring of support and sponsorship for the ride and for Toni's Kitchen. We raised thousands of dollars more than I'd hoped and a great deal of awareness about those in need in our community. I was also able to make some great ongoing friendships with many of the volunteers and guests there at TK's. (By the way, a portion of any proceeds from this book will also be contributed to Toni's Kitchen.)

Those issues settled, plans for the trip began in earnest. Establishing the route we would take, at least in theory, was an easy task. We didn't need to reinvent the wheel. Race Across America (RAAM) is an organization that holds an annual competition of incredibly avid bikers (one might even say rabid bikers because they literally race across the continent in 12 days, stopping only to sleep. Even eating is done on the fly!). RAAM publishes its entire cross-continental course on line with great detail. Thanks to them, we had a very well specified route in hand.

With a bit more difficulty, including lots of schedule juggling logistics, the plans for our departure also came together. It would be complicated. Our bicycles would be in place, securely bungee-corded to the 20-year-old RV (named Tiggie, as some sort of a variation for her brand name – Ticonderoga)) that would be our supply vehicle and home away from home. Bill would leave New Jersey on Thursday evening, March 16, 2009 with his 25-year-old son Jonathan, who would share the driving and then bike along with us for the first week of the trip. They would drive to Iowa by Friday evening to pick up Kriss and spend the night at his home, right on the banks of the Mississippi River in Le Claire. Saturday morning, the three of them would resume the drive westward.

The next day, Easter Sunday, I would be in the pulpit in the morning and then by late afternoon I'd be in the air, flying west from Newark to Las Vegas (yes, Las Vegas!) to meet up with the entourage. Bill, Jonathan and Kriss would arrive at the airport in Las Vegas just in time to pick up Dennis Barnum (Bill's brother-in-law, who would be our faithful supply driver for the first week) and me. Dennis and I both flew into Las Vegas from different origins, but were scheduled to arrive at approximately the same time. As unlikely as it may seem, everything went as planned!

You might think that Las Vegas would be a strange and wild place to begin our journey, but it wasn't. The glitzy casino/hotel where we spent the night really did have the cheapest rates in town. The truth is, by the time we landed I was exhausted from a very long and emotionally packed day, and from the many days and weeks of preparation leading up to it. Kriss and I had a bite of supper together and then I went directly to bed. The next morning the whole assemblage got up early, boarded Tiggie and resumed the last of the westward push to California.

We got to the coast just south of Carlsbad, California on Monday, April 20th. It was a little later in the afternoon than we had hoped but it was still in plenty of time to touch our wheels to the waters of the Pacific Ocean and begin to pedal east!

Finally, weeks and months after it was conceived, the trip was underway. What followed would be our journey from Carlsbad across the mountains, valleys, deserts, prairies, cities and towns of America. Forty-seven days later, we would touch our wheels to the waters of the Atlantic Ocean in Bowers Beach, Delaware, the end of our journey. A sampling of the experiences, observations and reflections that I had on the road make up the stuff of this book.

Shortly after returning home at the end of the trip, I was interviewed for the Public Radio program, "Spiritually Speaking." Host Linda Anderson of WVKR, the local NPR affiliate at Vassar College, asked me why I thought the theme of adventure journeys is so popular in literature, in movies and in so many genres. Why, she wondered, was it something so important in our culture, and why so important for me to undertake at this particular point in my life? I was ready for her question...

The adventure journey is a metaphor for life itself. I find myself in good company as many before me have mapped out the exploration of their internal lives while chronicling the narrative of their external experience. Homer tells of Odysseus' ever-interrupted journey. Dante scours the far regions of hell. Beowulf battles with men and monsters of the deep. Henry David Thoreau travels through the universe going no further than the environs of Walden Pond. Jack Kerouac finds himself amid his own antics against a mid 20th Century American backdrop. William Least Heat Moon finds himself in a world fused of nature and spirit... Charlie Ortman pedals his way towards connection and meaning while biking across the continent.

In a short and intense period of time the wanderer experiences myriad occurrences, opportunities and challenges that are something of a microcosm of the larger journey that is life. These individual adventurers and adventures present metaphors and lessons that are part of that larger metaphor. Sometimes metaphors become instantly clear; at other times they take a while to unpack.

Very often while on the trip, we'd start our day's ride, or start up again after a rest break, by mounting our bikes and shouting out a kind of charge. That way we'd all be mindfully and safely in sync with one another as we set out. So, one of us would trumpet our departure by hollering out something like, "We're rolling," or, "Head'em up and move'em out," or, "Moving on," or something like that. "Moving on," seemed like a good way to start a ride, just as it seems a good beginning and ending for many experiences in life. I use it through the book in cycling from one scenario to the next.

With a milestone birthday on the horizon and sabbatical time at my disposal, I was ready for some adventure, for some opportunities to test my strength, and to see what I might discover on the road. The thoughts expressed on the pages of this book are some gleanings that are the fruits of this venture. I have recorded them because I want to share a few of these metaphors, these lessons from the road that were a gift to me, with you. My hope is that they might have meaning for you, too. Or better yet, they might help to put you more in touch with some of your own experiences and observations along the road you are traveling. At any rate, I'm delighted to have you along.

Moving on...

"Life is like riding a bicycle. To keep your balance, you must keep moving."   -- Albert Einstein

Yes, I know, that's a simile and not a metaphor. Still, it leads to the thought that – in order to have balance at all, you got to begin first by moving.

My first lesson from this journey really began well before we ever hit the road. When I started to seriously contemplate even going on this bicycle trip, I contacted the only world-class bicyclist I know, Gary Sanderson. Gary is a high-end septuagenarian who can do just about anything. And he's a member of my congregation. He had made a cross-country trip himself and I asked for his advice. He shared a ton of important information about all kinds of things with me.

He taught me about the different kinds of chain oil and which one to use under what conditions. He taught me how to repair a broken chain. He told me I needed to carry extra spokes, which I would not have guessed, and how to carry them so that they'd be tucked out of the way. "You never know if you might need them," he suggested. He showed me many of the tools I'd need to have along and how to use them. He told me about the clothing I'd need, how to wear it, wash it and pack it.

His best advice though was, "The most important thing in planning a trip like this, Charlie, is deciding that you are go-ing to take it. Once you've made that decision, everything else will fall in place and help get you ready for it. The most important thing to know ahead of time is that you *are* going to do it," he stressed. "You *are going* to make this trip!"

I remember deciding to marry my wife, Judy, when I was 28

years old. I remember choosing with her to become a parent two years later. I remember answering my call to ministry several years later when our youngest daughter, Shana, was heading into kindergarten, when my tenure as an at-home-dad was coming to an end. I remember so many decisions that I've made throughout my life where I couldn't begin, ahead of time, to comprehend all the implications that would follow and fall into place.

There was always one assumption that I could appreciate though, especially in retrospect: whatever it was, the decision would not leave me standing still. I would be moving on. Relationships and circumstances would be changing; moving means change. Of course, moving also leaves open the possibility of falling down later on. Standing still though, is worse than falling down. It means never moving on from anything at all.

Mahatma Gandhi put it this way, "You may never know what results from your action, but if you do nothing there will be no action." Goethe said, "Whatever you can do, or dream you can, begin it. Boldness has genius, power, and magic in it." If there was going to be a ride, it had to begin with a committed idea of the ride.

"Okay," I said to Gary. "I'm going to do this. I'm going to ride my bike across the country!" Everything else that happened became possible in that one moment.

Moving on...

We got a much later start than we'd hoped on the first afternoon of the trip. Doesn't it always seem like things take about twice as long as you think they will! But at last we made it to Carlsbad. We slipped into our riding clothes, gathered our gear, and took our bikes down to the sandy shore so we could dip our wheels into the rolling waves of the Pacific Ocean. And then finally, finally we were off and riding! Yes, yes, yes!

There were thousands of miles ahead of us; the sun was shining as the pleasant ocean air rushed by us. I felt a kinship to all of the great explorers I'd studied back in school: Balboa, Ponce de León, Leif Eriksson and others. The world was there for me to find, mile-by-mile. I started counting them off – one, two, three... The climb from sea level started gradually through the northern San Diego suburbs. Before long we were pushing hard up the side of one of the San Marcos Mountains in western California.

I haven't mentioned what my greatest anxiety about the trip was in anticipation of it. I figured one way or another I could handle most of the challenges the road might offer. But I was not so confident in my ability to respond to threatening or bad drivers.

So there I was that first day, pedaling for all I was worth, up the winding mountain road. I thought I was doing pretty well when the driver of a semi truck decided to teach me a lesson about bicycling in California. He literally blew past me at about 60 miles per hour. I don't know, but I suspected that he knew there was less than a 12 to 18 inch margin between the side of his truck and my well-being.

Maybe you have been on a bike or even walking along the

side of the road when a big truck has passed you. The pull of gravity that holds us to the earth seems slight in comparison to the suction that pulls you in toward a fast-moving, big truck. I did not want to die... not on this very first day of the trip! Probably not later in it either, but I was staying focused in the moment. I could actually feel myself being pulled under the trailer. Somehow I immediately recognized that, if I acted at once, I had three options to choose from.

One, I could steer my bike away from the truck and into the rock-filled ditch on the side of the road. I immediately hated this idea. Although I didn't pause to think about it a lot, I knew that serious injury was likely and so was the possibility of totaling my bike. This still seemed better than if I fell in front of the rear tires of the truck, though.

Two, I could stop pedaling and slow down. If I could focus all my attention and my muscles towards maintaining the margin between me and the truck, I might be able to fight off the pull that would be my sure end. If I could squeeze hard enough, I might be able to hold my course. I would just have to hold on to my bike and whatever ground I could until the truck got past me.

Three, I could reach out with my left hand and try to keep myself from the suction by pushing against the truck. Maybe I could maintain my distance from it at arm's length. Injury was not certain this way, but it did seem likely.

None of the choices seemed to be outrageously viable. I opted for number two. I ended up squeezing all of my muscles so hard trying to hold ground that they ached for a long while afterwards. I've had a number of close calls in my lifetime, but I don't think any of them were closer than this. I'm quite glad that I'm still around to tell the tale.

How often in our lives, I wonder, when faced with major challenges, do we feel that we *are* being *sucked in* by forces beyond our control?   The truth is that the pull of those forces probably really is beyond our control, but our responses to them are not. It's up to us. We may or may not emerge from the situation unscathed, but whatever we choose to do, we are determining outcomes that might impact on us and those around us in significant ways. We might live with the results the rest of our lives. Depending on the situation, that may or may not be a long time!

British education consultant, Elaine Maxwell, writes:
   "My will shall shape the future. Whether I fail or succeed shall be no [one's] doing but my own. I am the force; I can clear any obstacle before me or I can be lost in the maze.
My choice; my responsibility; win or lose, only I hold the key to my destiny."
Being passive or doing nothing at all, is an act of will that has consequences as sure as any other action we might take. Sometimes we do well to choose while the choosing is good – good for ourselves and for those around us. And sometimes it's scary as hell, no matter what we do!

Moving on... but not too far...

I want to say a bit more about drivers from the perspective of a bicyclist. From my view of having now biked over 3,000 miles on the highways and byways of this country, there seem to be three groups of drivers. The first and largest includes those drivers who see cyclists and do whatever they can to provide an adequate and safe margin for them as they pass around. The folks in this group range all the way from those who honk and wave and shout encouragement to those who simply, quietly and adequately make their way around the cyclist.

The smallest group includes those drivers who also go well out of their way for bikers, but who do so, like the semi truck driver in California, in order to teach bikers a lesson. They cut their margins short, if there is a margin at all. Members of this group also often honk and wave and shout but their gestures have a very different meaning. You can just tell.

The third group really doesn't go out of its way for cyclists in any particular direction. In fact, it's as if they are unaware that there are even cyclists on the road. They are sort of in their own world, on cell phones, daydreaming, or whatever. Sometimes they are less dangerous than the second nasty group, but they still pose a serious threat to those of us pedaling along on the side of the road.

It's too easy to think that people fall neatly into only one of these three categories. I suspect that most of us typically flow in and out of all three of them at various times. I know that I do. Still, it strikes me that these groups provide a useful metaphor relating to generosity.

There are different periods or stages in our lives when our

own generosity might be well described as being like any of the three groups: sometimes we are generous and eager to share what we have with others. Other times we are miserly and unwilling to give an inch or anything else. And then there are times when most of us get overly self-absorbed, when we are unaware of the needs of the world and others around us. I have to think that the larger good is well served when we are paying attention though, when we respond to what we experience with generosity. I know that at least bicyclists are well served by attention and generosity on the part of drivers.

Former First Lady Barbara Bush got it right when she said, "Giving frees us from the familiar territory of our own needs by opening our mind to the unexplained worlds occupied by the needs of others."

Moving on...

In the early days of the trip I had a lot of equipment issues. In the midst of all that though, I didn't even recognize that the equipment was my problem. That took a while to discover. At first, I thought it was just me...

I'd been assured by a number of people in the know that, "Nobody is in the kind of condition they need to be in for a cross-continental bike trip until about two weeks into it." Not being a particularly great athlete, I thought it would take me *at least* a couple of weeks to get into shape. I've also always been told that, "It's a poor worker who blames his tools." So I expected the first couple of weeks to be challenging. But my experience far exceeded my expectations.

To say that I had equipment issues is a serious understatement. My custom built bicycle, a Lynski, is one of the best made in this country. However, my riding shoes and pedals actually ended up injuring my feet. My saddle, otherwise known as a bike seat, was particularly well-suited for racing, but not necessarily for long-distance touring. *The thought of that narrow little perch still brings a tear to my eye and a pang of discomfort to my tush.*

I also had a problem with oversized tires that occasionally rubbed against the frame. Believe me, you don't want anything rubbing against anything else when you're riding an average of 70 to 80 miles each day. The gearing on my bike was very well set up for riding on flat terrain and for racing, but not necessarily for hours or days on end of biking in the mountains.

So, I didn't know at first that these were the issues. Despite weeks of focused training, I fully trusted at the onset of the trip that I was not in good shape. I figured I needed to tough it out for a while. Blaming my tools was not an option, until I could ride no further. That's when I met Cindy Alwards who ran High Gear Bike Shop in Prescott, Arizona. "You are really doing a lot of damage to your feet," she gasped as she looked into my shoes and found the source of my foot problems.

"Oh," I said. "Maybe we should take look at some of this other stuff, too." Eventually I swapped out the shoes and pedals, the tires and the seat. The gears I learned to live with. Things improved significantly. Chicago singer and songwriter Tom Dundee wrote, "Expectations we have can lead down the path where that devil discouragement lives."

It seems that sometimes in our lives we have great expectations of how things are going to be. And then our experiences become our teachers. Smack! They bring us quickly into a new relationship with reality.

If we're going to stay upright on our bicycles, or forthright in our lives, we have to adapt. If we want to keep moving on, we have to apply what we learn through experience to the choices we make going forward. And when we fail to adapt, we run the risk of seriously crippling ourselves.

Another thing – sometimes in our lives, wise and generous people provide us an awareness of what has worked well for *them*. We can learn a lot from knowledgeable and caring people, but the truth is – we *are not* them; we can't ever *be* them. What has worked for them might or might not be what works well for us. Perhaps what we can learn from them though, are ways *to discover* what might work well for us. That alone is an enormous gift.

Transcendentalist and Unitarian, Ralph Waldo Emerson, put

it this way in 1838, when he addressed a class of graduating seminarians in his Harvard Divinity School address: "Cast behind you all conformity and acquaint [yourself], at first-hand, with Deity. Go alone, refuse the good models and dare to love God without mediator or veil. The time is coming when all [people] will see that the gift of God to the soul is... a sweet, natural goodness..."

If each of us is going to get the most out of life, I suspect we'll each need to wear shoes that fit us... and not somebody else's.

Moving on...

... Dateline: Julian, California, April 15, 2009
(CBO Press International)

A small group of bicycling enthusiasts rode into this mountaintop village at 3:30 yesterday afternoon. They had spent much of their day making little progress along the way on their cross-continental biking trek. Reportedly, they had spent much of the day dealing with minor mechanical issues, which had caused several delays. As they neared this mountain refuge, along with them came a dramatic change in weather. Within only a half-hour after their arrival, temperatures plummeted some 30 degrees. An implacable, pea soup fog settled in, winds gusted up to 50 mph, and intermittent sleeting rain mixed with snow began pelting the town.

The cyclists, unable to reach their supply driver by cell phone, eventually settled into Margarita's Mexican Restaurant for the evening. There they found shelter, as well as nourishment and spiritual sustenance. A witness at the restaurant reported having heard one of the cyclists comment, "Wow, is this something, or what?!" By evening's end, another witness reported, that the driver of the team's RV had relocated the bikers and, gathering them in, put them to bed for the night.

As dawn broke this morning, a more seasonably temperate day began in Julian. The cyclists departed town in their RV hoping to locate a bicycle repair shop in nearby Ramona. There they hoped to get some further modifications still required by one of the bicycles, prior to resuming their coast-to-coast pedaling journey. "We don't know how long it will take," one of the riders reported. "We only know that we're going to get there."

Do you ever wonder how other people see you? I do.

Sometimes I care very much about how I might be perceived, other times not so much. I don't need to be addicted to public opinion, but I do want to have an idea of how I am perceived by those around me. I really kind of like it when people like me. I can get along without that when I need to, but I like it better the other way. No man is an island and all of that.

When Bill and I wandered into Margarita's Mexican Restaurant late that afternoon in Julian, peels of hysterical laughter from Margarita's Mom, who was running the place, greeted us. We later learned that *Mom* – whose real name we never did learn – was in charge because Margarita was in the hospital battling a serious illness.

Mom, the proprietress de jour and a local patroness with whom she'd been visiting, laughed out loud at the sight of us until tears were rolling down their cheeks and they were holding onto their sides. We tried to act nonchalant as we walked in and sat down. We suspected their response was maybe because we looked kind of silly in our biking shorts, shirts and shoes, when everyone else in town was wearing parkas.

"We've been hearing about you guys for over an hour," Margarita's Mom said. "You've been the talk of the town! And now we can see why. You look like a couple of soggy puppies! You sure aren't dressed for being out in this weather!"

Once she stopped laughing and heard our story, Margarita's Mom saw that we were feeling like a pair of fools. She grabbed us a couple of Negra Modelo beers. Then she made it quite clear that we were welcome to stay as long as we wanted or needed to. When Kriss and Jonathan arrived, freezing cold, a little while later, they were warmly greeted, too. But they didn't get nearly the reception that Bill and I had benefited so much from. I guess they weren't quite the novelty we'd been.

Garrison Keillor once quipped, "I believe in looking reality straight in the eye and denying it." Try as we might to see ourselves as a crew of swarthy, engaging world travelers, we appeared to Margarita's Mom and her friend more nearly as a bunch of cold, tired and ill-prepared vagabonds who needed a warm dry place to come in from the cold, wet and foggy storm to hang out for a while.

M. Scott Peck, wrote in, *The Road Less Traveled*, "The truth is that our finest moments are most likely to occur when we are feeling deeply uncomfortable, unhappy, or unfulfilled. For it is only in such moments, propelled by our discomfort, that we are likely to step out of our ruts and start searching for different ways or truer answers."

The bicycle trek itself was a long journey into a whole series of *finer* moments for me. I was often uncomfortable, frequently unhappy and always in search of fulfillment. Margarita's Mom helped me to take another look at myself through a new lens. She helped me step out of the rooted images I had of myself and gain a less serious and more enjoyable view of me and of my challenging situation. The hot enchiladas and cold beer were a nice touch, too.

Moving on...

Riding a bicycle in the mountains isn't like riding anywhere else. I should tell you that I'm originally from the Midwest, the land of enormous skies and endless horizons. Back home in parts of Illinois, on a very clear day, it's said that sometimes you can look far off into the distant horizon and actually see... the back of your own head!

That's not the way it is in the mountains. In the mountains you're typically riding either uphill or downhill. If you're riding downhill, the horizon is generally some low point where the road stops going down and starts going back up. If you're going uphill, chances are that the horizon is still not too far off in the distance in that direction either. You just follow the rise of the hill up to where it meets a not-too-distant sky. Then your view is all downhill again.

Climbing mountains on a bicycle is arduous, at the least. After a while, I became sure that I would spend the remainder of my life, however long it might last, pedaling uphill. Early in our journey I found myself climbing a steep long mountain hill, begrudging any of its downhill segments. They only meant that I'd have to re-climb whatever altitude I lost in the descent. I would eventually have to make up the loss on my way back up to the summit where I was heading in the first place. I didn't need the additional debt incurred as a result of the short-lived plunge.

Let's say you're heading for a pass that is at 12,000 feet. It takes a lot of effort to climb 1,000 feet, by the way. So, let's say you get up to 10,000 feet and you have 2,000' yet to go. You pedal up around the next bend only to find yourself in a rapid descent of maybe a couple of thousand feet. Now here you are again at 4,000' below top of the pass. And you have to start climbing the lost 2000' all over again. It didn't seem right! And it didn't seem to make efficient use of my very limited energies and abilities!

I found myself loathing these drops in elevation. Finally though, I recognized that the elevation of the mountain passes had little to do with my journey towards them. Those mountains existed a long time before I arrived on the scene. The dips and rises were there and will stay there for a long time to come. The rises are always going to be a challenge to the likes of people like me.

But that didn't mean that the effortless downhill stretches that were interspersed among the climbs had to be a drag. They weren't a drag at all. They were a very easy part of the ride that allowed me to just coast along, at least for a while. They weren't an encumbrance to the climb at all; they were merely a part of the ride.

I wonder how often in our lives, when we somehow manage to find ourselves in a downhill moment or on a momentarily less demanding path, do we forget to appreciate the respite, and instead keep our focus on the challenges yet to come? And besides, who's to say that the mountaintop is the journey's end anyway?

Riding a bike through the mountains is much like walking a labyrinth. Labyrinths are mazelike patterns of passageways that people often walk through as part of a spiritual exercise. If you've walked on one, you know how quickly, in the beginning, you find yourself heading for the final, central heart of the labyrinth – only to be led far away from it by a circuitous route. That longer course leads through countless more steps and a lot more experience before the center of the labyrinth is ever finally reached.

Often when biking in the mountains, you can be so sure that

the rise you're currently climbing is the one that leads to the very top of the pass. You're absolutely confident that you can see that what's coming next is the ultimate height of the mountain. It's just ahead of you, just around the next bend... Then you make that next turn, and you see once more that you're heading downhill again, before going up again, before going down again. And finally, you move ahead through the newly discovered terrain until you can see what looks like, *yes maybe it is,* only one more rise still to go. And so it goes...

There are many similarities between the labyrinth of biking in the mountains and life itself. It really isn't over until it's over. And who *is* to say, until we have some perspective on it all, whether the most meaningful experiences are those moments spent in the heights, or even in the depths of our being, or if they are in the transitions between the two.

Poet Alvin Fein wrote one of my favorite poems about life as such a journey. Here are a few lines of it:

Birth is a beginning
And death a destination
But life is a journey,
A going --- a growing
From stage to stage...

Until, looking backward or ahead,
We see that victory lies
Not at some high place
along the way,
But in having made the journey,
stage by stage
A sacred pilgrimage.

Moving on...

If you want to have a snowball fight with someone, make sure they want to have one too!

My traveling companions and I were riding our bikes through the Rocky Mountains of northern New Mexico, not far from Taos. We were all fairly well spread out along our route according to our abilities. Of course, that meant that I was way at the back of the pack as we climbed towards the top of Bob Cat Pass at nearly 10,000 feet. It would prove to be one of the most challenging climbs of the entire trip. For me, it was brutal. There were countless switchbacks with very steep rises between each of them. Not only the incredible panoramas that were constantly in view were breathtaking, so was the lack of oxygen in the thin air of the high altitude.

At an event at Toni's Kitchen, back before I'd left on the trip, a woman had said to me, "I'm very concerned about you riding through those mountains." I assured her that she was not alone in her concern. I suspected during it, that the climb up to Bob Cat Pass was just the sort of "*concerned*" experience that both she and I had had in mind.

So I found myself riding up the snow-banked road, straining for all I was worth, both in my legs, as I struggled to keep pumping forward, and in my lungs, as I struggled to keep pumping oxygen into my bloodstream. I would push myself as hard as I could, only to get as far as a few hundred yards. Then I would stop, catch my breath, rest my legs and push forward again. I'd ride for another few hundred yards and then rest again. The pattern repeated itself for hours. You don't get very far very fast riding like that. At least I didn't. My companions Bill and Kriss fared much better and for all I knew, they were hours ahead of me.

Slow as I might have been in my ascent, eventually, I sensed that I was nearing the top of the pass. There were even road signs that promised it was coming. They said, "Caution, Nearing Summit: Oncoming Traffic." As far as I was concerned, they could have said, "The End Is Near!" Oftentimes, when you're near the very top of a pass like that, things start getting easier. The pitch of the grade eases and you can finish the climb in fine form.

Not this time. The ascent was vicious to the very end. My feet, clipped to the pedals, were barely going around, as my legs pushed against them with what felt like the very last shred of strength they could muster. My lungs felt like they were ready to burst, as they tried to keep up with my body's demand for oxygen. All I could do was, all I could think was – pump, breathe, pump, breathe...

As I drew within a couple of hundred feet of the summit, I saw a person walking along the side of the road. I recognized that it was a woman we'd met earlier on the trip. She was smiling at me as our paths approached one another. As best I could, I attempted to smile back, all the while still thinking – pump, breathe, pump, breathe...

And then I watched in horror as her hands came out from behind her back. She grinned broadly, as she pelted me with two ice balls she'd dug out of the snow bank. One hit me in the face and the other went into my chest. I was in total disbelief. I was *sore afraid* (yes, I mean *sore afraid*, it's a biblical reference) that I was going to fall right over on the bike. My feet were still clipped tight and I didn't think I had enough additional strength to execute the snap movement required to get them out. I really was scared almost to death. All I could say to her was, "Don't do that. Please don't do that to me, especially *not now*." But it was already done.

I know in the larger scheme of things this is not a big deal, but I really was horrified. I suppose when you're almost 60 years old and you've just pushed yourself to your absolute physical limit, you're not in the same frame of mind you might be, say, in other less threatening situations.

Turns out that the woman had spoken with Kriss and Bill earlier, as they'd passed through. She'd been expecting me, and she thought it would be fun to have a little welcoming party. What she had failed to take into consideration though, was me. She was up for a party and she didn't notice that I was barely up at all.

I said this wasn't a big deal and it wasn't. But I think this experience might be a good illustration of how things often breakdown between people in the world. Individuals acting in their own self-interest sometimes fail to consider the consequences that those interests have on others. Failure to consider the well-being of others, at its extreme, I think is the basis of evil. Evil is no more than human behavior, which promotes separation and suffering. Goodness on the other hand, which is also a human action, promotes healing.

Máiread Corrigan Maguire knows plenty about this subject. She is the co-founder of the Community of Peace People, an organization that attempts to encourage peaceful resolutions in troubled areas of the world, as she did in Northern Ireland. Along with her partner Betty Williams, she was co-recipient of the 1976 Nobel Peace Prize. Corrigan Maguire wrote:
"We frail humans are at one time capable of the greatest good and, at the same time, capable of the greatest evil. Change will only come about when each of us takes up the daily struggle ourselves to be more forgiving,

compassionate, loving, and above all joyful in the knowledge that, by some miracle of grace, we can change as those around us can change too."

So there I was at the top of Bob Cat Pass, looking straight into the face of my need to forgive someone for having done me wrong. I'd have rather not had that opportunity altogether, but I didn't really have any choice in the matter. My only choice was to decide the way in which I would respond. It might have been helpful had I received an apology from my ice ball hurling assailant, but that didn't happen either. I was left with the option of being either spiteful or of forgiving her. It took me a little while to get through that one.

There's lots of counsel out there on this one, though. "The weak can never forgive. Forgiveness is the attribute of the strong," wrote Mohandas Gandhi. James Baldwin concluded that, "Nobody is more dangerous than he who imagines himself pure in heart, for his purity, by definition, is unassailable."

In the end, I knew that I, too, am all too often overly self-centered and careless when it comes to the well-being of others. I don't want to be, but sometimes... I am. I also knew that in order for me to do the best I can in my life, I have to be able to forgive myself so that I can move on.

If I have to forgive myself for the sake of my own well-being, then I guess I needed to figure out a way to forgive this woman, too. She didn't have to think that she needed my forgiveness in order from me to forgive her. And she didn't think that. At least she didn't let on that she did.

Besides, I didn't want to become who I would have to be in order to carry the burden of bitterness. It had already been a tough enough day. Climbing the mountains on my bike was burden enough!

Post Script... It's not like me to be wasteful of perfectly good experiences. So, after returning home, I shared this story with my congregation, as an illustration in a sermon. I was approached a couple of weeks later by a youngish woman named Silke, who had emigrated from Germany a number of years ago when she was even more youngish. Silke told me about how, after she graduated from university in Germany years earlier, she had gone on a hiking and climbing trek in the Himalayan Mountains of India with a number of other people. About two weeks into the journey she said they were climbing a summit that was over 16,000 feet.

They had been making their way up the mountain for several days and she said that her experience had become similar to my own ascent of Bob Cat Pass. The group would hike about 200 yards and then, breathless and with throbbing legs, they would stop to rest. Then they would go the next couple hundred yards and stop again. She said she could really relate to my experience.

"Then," she said, "... on the last day of the ascent, I decided that I was not going to stop every 200 yards. I was just going to walk right through the pain and through the fear of not being able to breathe. And I was just going to keep going and see what happened."
"And what did happen," I asked?

"I just kept going," she said. "After a while my legs didn't hurt any more, and even though I had to keep breathing as hard as I could, I kept breathing. And I made it all the way to the top without stopping!"

"Wow," I asked, "what was the payback?"

"There wasn't any," she answered. "When I got to the top, I had the most euphoric experience of my life. I could see all the way down two long mountain ranges, and out across some of the most beautiful landscape in the world. I was in heaven. Sometime you should try it," she said. "When you think you can't go any further, you might want to try to see if you can. Just keep going!"

The gauntlet has been thrown. Now I guess I have a good reason to start planning my next expedition.

Moving on...

"Beauty is unbearable, drives us to despair, offering us for a moment the glimpse of an eternity that we should like to stretch out over the whole of time."   -- Albert Camus

Flashback... I remember, from what seems an altogether different lifetime, a set of experiences that I once had in the Rocky Mountains. The year was 1974 and I was 24. The divorce that I had just endured had been brutal, not for the all too typical reasons of malicious gouging or anything like that. It had been so difficult because it was not a part of my nature to go back on vows that I have made. The choice to end the marriage had not been mine. I really was at the time quite psychologically prepared to be married, "... until death do us part."

And so, as I found myself adjusting to single life, I was something of a psychological and emotional mess. In those days I often found myself going out from my home in Chicago to Denver. There I spent indulgent time in the healing household of my brother and sister-in-law. Bill and Elaine took me in and offered me the time and space I needed while attempting to put my life back together. They both worked regular jobs and, as long as I could get her to work and pick her up on time, I was usually welcome to use Elaine's VW Beetle convertible during the day.

I would often drive up into the mountains with the top down, totally taken by the beauty of Colorado. Sometimes I'd find a trail and take a hike. Sometimes I would just drive along, stopping from time to time at little pullovers, marked with signs that read, "Vista." I didn't have any particular goals or ambitions for myself during those days. I just wanted to get through what I was going through. It was hard.

I remember one afternoon in particular. I was driving along, up at a fairly high altitude. I came around a bend in the road and found myself stunned, looking way out over what seemed like the whole world. I pulled off at the Vista sign, parked the Beetle, got out and walked over to the rock wall that held me comfortably and safely over the vast abyss below.

Looking out over one of the most spectacular visual experiences in my entire lifetime, I was filled with awe and appreciation. Right before me were the purple mountains majesty, great forests of trees, deep lush valleys and sprightly serpentine streams. It went on forever. I could see that the world was a thing of magnificent beauty and that somehow I was a part of that incredible splendor. It was so beautiful that I ached from it.

And then, on an impulse based on countless experiences before, I turned to the person next to me to say, "My God! Isn't this the most beautiful thing you've ever seen?" Then all of a sudden I was yanked, almost violently, back into the reality of my broken life. There was no person standing next to me at that Vista. I was quite alone, all by myself.

The pang of emptiness that instantly struck throughout my entire body was at least as great in intensity as what I had just experienced in the opposite direction from the grandeur of the mountains. My emotional state plummeted from that high peak to the lowest chasm. My world went from incredibly awesome to devastatingly awful in a split moment. I was in agony and I did not know how I was going to survive.

This one moment, even now, strikes me as having been perhaps the most difficult one in my entire life. The beauty had indeed become unbearable. It had certainly driven me to despair. There had been a glimpse of the grandeur of eternity, which then stood in contrast with my own misery. I could not imagine any connection that would allow me to span the gap from the one world to the other.

Over the course of the next several years, little by little, I was able to gather together some of the pieces that allowed me to begin my life again. It was not easy and I didn't always know that I would make it. Going to restaurants and to the movies alone became the way that I gauged my progress. In the beginning, I felt so conspicuous and out of place and alone. As time went by though, I began to learn to enjoy the pleasure of my own company.

Poet Maya Angelou wrote, "I long, as does every human being, to be home where ever I find myself." There is a heart rending Zulu chant, *Thula Klizeo*, written by South African Joseph Shabalala when he was on a trip from his homeland to New York City back in 1988. "Thula Klizeo nala pasa kaya," go the words. "Be still my heart, for even here I am at home." The journey is ever to find that place within, which makes our home without.

Flash forward... Many years and several visits later, I again found myself traveling through the peaks and valleys of the Rocky Mountains. This time I crossed the Rockies in New Mexico. It was from the eleventh through the fifteenth days of my bicycle pilgrimage across the country. It was a trek similar in character, I suspect, to that of Ponce de León's centuries earlier – it was an effort to find youthfulness in my somewhat more than middle-aged body.

It was a very different experience than the one I had nearly 35 years earlier. Repeatedly during this part of the trip, my riding companions and I would come upon breathtaking vistas that again were filled with purple mountains majesty, with forests and valleys, and seemingly endless splendor. Yet again the mountains were awesome and awe inspiring.

This time though, I would turn to Bill or Kriss, whoever was nearest, and exclaim with unbounded joy, "Good God, can you believe that!" It was believable. And it was wonderful, too.

But even more, there was someone back home. It was someone who cared that I was on this journey altogether, someone who cared that my experience was so splendid. I would often try to call Judy on my cell phone at those spectacular moments, just to share with her the incredible things that I could see. Sometimes the calls would go through and sometimes they wouldn't. It didn't matter though, at least not too much. I would be able to tell her eventually, and I could show her the thousands of pictures that Bill was taking all along the way.

To me, it's hugely important to share my life with someone that I love. It's hugely important that my wife Judy is that person in my life. In so many ways she has saved my life over and over again.

The difference between the earlier experience and this recent one, besides the fact that I was way older, is that I had learned to hold the many pieces, oftentimes broken pieces, of my life together. Love is the glue that has done that holding.

I've learned that life is not perfect. I, myself, am a long ways from perfect. I don't even like the word *perfect*. It's an idea that has no place in reality.

There are moments though, moments of wholeness. Wholeness does not exist as an approximation of perfection. It exists as a result of gathering together all the many pieces that are the parts of our lives, and then holding those pieces together. Wholeness is finding *in those moments* not only the pain and suffering, but the beauty and the splendor that are a part of every life. It is the process of finding who we are in relationship with *all-that-is*, and then accepting that whole as precious.

American painter and novelist, Henry Miller, aptly noted that, "The moment one gives close attention to anything, even a blade of grass, it becomes a mysterious, awesome, indescribably magnificent world in itself." If a blade of grass contains such magnificence, how blessed are we by bike rides and mountain vistas, by art and music, by those we love and even by those whom we have loved.

I don't know how my life would have turned out had Judy not become a part of it. I have to say that I feel so very fortunate that she is a part of it and that I don't have to know otherwise. Together we share the glue that holds together, not only each of our lives, but both of them. And more, we share the glue that holds our lives together with the lives of our three incredible, grown children, who themselves now venture into the world to discover their own heartbreaks and moments of salvation, their own moments of wholeness.

One of the many things that come to mind when standing high above a phenomenal mountain scene, or working within a relationship that endures, is gratitude. "Good God! Can you believe that?" My heart is filled with gratitude, and it is a gratitude that must be expressed.

Albert Einstein, who was as much a philosopher as he was a scientific genius, articulated my feelings quite nearly when he said, "I don't try to imagine a personal god; it suffices to stand in awe at the structure of the world, insofar as it allows our inadequate senses to appreciate it."

Beauty alone can be devastating. But when we move from beauty to awe, from awe to gratitude, from gratitude to service, we are gathering the pieces together. We are gaining more than just a glimpse of an eternity. What we are gathering is something of value that can indeed be stretched out over the whole of a lifetime.

In the end I suppose the gratitude I feel for being a part of this creation can only be expressed in my service to it. I am so fortunate to have opportunities to serve in ways that continue to supply untold quantities of glue. I am blessed by the love that holds my life together, as it is shaped into the whole that it is becoming.

Moving on...

Nicknames are labels that we don't confer upon ourselves. Nicknames are given to us by others and have to do with how we are seen by those others. Sometimes they are flattering and often times, when given by those who love us, they can be very endearing. Sometimes though, they're not so flattering at all, and they can even be something of an embarrassment.

I've gone through life using my nickname Charlie as the primary representation of my identity. My first name is actually Charles, but it's pretty rare that anyone who knows me at all calls me that. When I was a kid, if my mother called me by my given name Charles, I laid low because I knew I was about to get it. But when she sang the song, *Charlie, Me Boy* (btw, she was an excellent soprano), I felt like there was nowhere else on earth I'd rather be, other than right there by her side, soaking it in. In my professional life, the use of my nickname Charlie seems to create an atmosphere of comfort and accessibility for people, which I think serves my ministry well.

As a kid, I had two other nicknames that I was sometimes called by classmates. One of them I liked. The other not so much.

By anyone's standards, I'm from a very large family – there were ten of us Ortman kids. Every morning before school, my mother would make our lunches and line them up on the kitchen counter near the back door. They were packed neatly in brown paper bags, which she had inscribed with each of our names. We would reuse those bags day after day until they were so crumpled that you could hardly read the names on them.

One morning on my way out of the house, I happen to grab the wrong bag. At lunchtime someone noticed that I was eating from a bag labeled, *Susie Ortman*. For years after that, when any of the guys in my class wanted to tease me for any reason at all, I would be called *Susie*. You might remember the Johnny Cash song, "How do you do, my name is Sue." It really was quite like that! While I loved my sister dearly and still do, I hated being called by her name.

Another nickname that I was sometimes known by at school was, *Orty*. It wasn't terribly clever and it wasn't outrageously enduring. Still, I liked it. It assumed a certain familiarity on the part of the user and I enjoyed being the recipient of that assumption. "Hey, Orty, go out for a long one," somebody might say in a football huddle.

"You bet," I'd answer gladly, feeling like a part of the team.

As we rode our bikes across the country, Bill, Kriss and I learned a lot about each other. We discovered a lot about who and how we were, together as a team. It didn't take very long for us to develop nicknames for one another. It's not that we used them all the time, but from time to time we would. It's not like we thought having nicknames was a good idea and so we went ahead and made them up. They just sort of came up naturally.

When you're involved in such an intense journey like we were, living in close quarters and enduring such an epic adventure together, it was easy for us to feel quite connected. We were each a part of the team. Our nicknames helped us to experience that connection and gave us a way of articulating it. The nicknames gave us a way of bonding, while acknowledging our very different roles on the team.

Bill is short like me, but quite wiry and deceptively strong. As I've mentioned, he is an incredible athlete. He could leave our starting point on many mornings, well after Kriss and I, and then, miles up the road, he would easily join back up with us again. "What a great morning this is," he would greet us with a big smile as he caught up. He'd just pedal along, seemingly without much of an effort at all.

Sometimes he would even take side trips to see a monument or some other thing of interest. It might be close by or several miles off of our path. Once, when we were riding across the Panhandle of Oklahoma, he took a detour of about ten miles so that he could pedal across the border into Texas. Kriss and I never knowingly strayed from the course. We had no interest in pedaling any amount of miles that weren't about getting us any closer to the East Coast. Bill wouldn't give it a second thought though. And always he'd catch up to us smiling away, breezing along just as easy as you please.

It didn't take long for Kriss and I to give Bill the nickname of *Jackrabbit*. No matter how fast he was going, Bill still had loads of energy in reserve. Whenever he wanted, he could kick into another gear and pour on the steam. Whether we were in flat lands or hills, didn't seem to matter. *Jackrabbit* was just right for Bill.

A bit later in the trip though, Kriss chose to re-dub Bill with another nickname. It was one that we sometimes, but sparingly, used. Bill really was like a jackrabbit, quickly darting about, often quite unpredictably. Add to that the tendency he often had of paying attention to all kinds of other things, even while riding his bike. He might take pictures while riding along. He might make or take a telephone calls. Sometimes he would even read his e-mail on his Blackberry while riding.

It was utterly amazing, but sometimes it would make Bill a little less aware of things around him than either Kriss or I would be comfortable with. It often made us feel quite concerned for his safety. A number of times he came very close to colliding with moving or even stationary objects. The most remarkable thing of all was that he never actually did. With his incredible athletic ability, he would pull out of a near disaster at the very last second.

That prompted Kriss to come up with, and I had to agree, the additional label that we sometimes used for Bill after a close call, which was, *Unsafe at Any Speed*. "Oh," he would smile, nodding his head when we used that name, "I probably should pay closer attention." Yeah-ha!

Kriss is very lanky and lean. He's also an excellent athlete. As a youth, he was a long-distance runner and he played both football and basketball. He continued with sports well into his adult years. His long-distance running is what stood him in good stead for our bike trip. He had incredible strength and endurance for the long haul. He could start riding at a very good clip in the morning, and continue along at the same pace indefatigably all day long. Even going up and down hills didn't seem to impede the consistency of his pedal stroke. He would just gear down a little lower, ride on a little slower, but pedal at about the same number of RPMs as ever.

Bill and I dubbed Kriss, *Even Steven*. His personality contained the same kind of level, under-spoken smoothness. Lots of times in heavy traffic, Bill and I would get all excited and bothered by drivers who were less than courteous and careful around bicycles. Sometimes we would even yell not so pleasant things at them. Not Kriss though. He would ride along in his even stride, his even temperament intact, keeping his attention focused on what he was doing. He is one of the smoothest characters, the steadiest people, the most *Even Steven* I've ever known.

I am built on a short frame, close to the ground as they say. My rather squat German legs are a bit more like tree trunks than they are limbs for fast or long-distance movement. My own athletic prowess – *a rather oxymoronic descriptor when related to me* – paled greatly in comparison with my riding companions. For the most part though, Kriss and Bill were very patient with me. My slowness didn't seem to be a problem for them. If it was, they did a gracious job of not letting on. It was, as you might imagine, a bit more difficult for me to deal with.

I sometimes referred to myself as, *The Weak Link*. Fortunately though, like I said earlier, we don't give ourselves nicknames. They are given to us. My friends *Jackrabbit* and *Even Steven* were bighearted. They chose not to attribute my less than benevolent, self-imposed moniker to me.

For reasons that I omit out of a sense of decorum, other than to say that my gastrointestinal processes are themselves the stuff of legend, Bill and Kriss referred to me lovingly and endearingly throughout our trip as, *The Gas Man*. You know what? That worked just fine for me. I felt loved and hey, I was part of the gang!

In, *Anam Cara: A Book of Celtic Wisdom*, the late Irish poet and philosopher, John O'Donohue wrote, "The hunger to belong is not merely a desire to be attached to something. It is rather sensing that great transformation and discovery become possible when belonging is sheltered and true."

Human beings are social animals, some of us more so than others, but we will all find our communities. We want to be attached. Sometimes we want to be connected with another person, sometimes with a group, sometimes with all or part of nature. If we are thoughtful and intentional in choosing our company, we will indeed find entry to transformation and discovery.

I would be quick to add that we don't always get to do the choosing. Sometimes we are chosen, by birth, by assignment or other means, to belong to groups not of our own making, and sometimes not even to our liking. Then it is up to each of us to be all the more intent on promoting shelter and truth, so that our participation, in whatever group it might be, can help to provide or to create the experience of transformation and discovery, both for ourselves and for others.

John O'Donohue went on:
"We should never allow our fears or the expectations of others to set the frontiers of our destiny... It is strange to be here. The mystery never leaves you alone. Behind your image, below your words, above your thoughts, the silence of another world waits. A world lives within you. No one else can bring you news of this inner world."

We have a need to let ourselves be held in the care and attention of others. The nourishment we gain from those connections sets us free to engage with the news of that inner world. Our inner selves have expression through our interactions with others; our lives are made manifest, as we discover how our inner and outer worlds are interconnected. And while we do well to care and to be cared for, we need not be limited by those we are in relationship with. We can accept what they have to offer us, learn from it, make meaning of it, and then continue to choose for ourselves who it is we are becoming.

What we call ourselves and each other, our names and our nicknames, afford us a sense of identity and belonging in our circles of kinship. What we call others can do more than include or exclude them. It can inform and enlighten them. It can provide them warning, safety or affirmation.

What others call us can do the same for us in return. What we are called can cause us to question our worth and our sense of belonging. Or it can help us towards and give us support in our quest for the discovery and transformation that is waiting to unfold in our lives. We each get to be the finders and makers of meaning within our relationships and within our lives. We don't do this in isolation, but in communion with those we are connected to. This seems like good enough reason to come up with all the endearing and embracing nicknames that we can find for those who are in our lives. Who'd have thought that nicknames could pave the way to a better world!

This is the *Gas Man*, signing off for now.

Moving on...

We began our 16th day in Springer, New Mexico, setting out early because the weather was supposed to start out ugly and then get worse as the day wore on. We rode out along Maxwell Avenue, heading up toward the highway on the edge of town. Even at the beginning, we rode through a pea soup fog punctuated by driving rain. As we rode past the electronic marquee in front of the Farmer's and Cattleman's International Bank, it said that it was 42 degrees at 6:30 AM. "Oh, my God," I mumbled a quiet prayer to myself.

The weather forecast did not let us down. Things got...well, they did not get any better. The challenges were many. It was cold and rainy. I was soaked to the bone and freezing cold. My eyeglasses were dripping wet, inside and out, and all fogged up, so that I had to take them off, which is not a particularly excellent thing for me to do. And to top it off there was a strong headwind that put my progress into very slow motion. You might have had dreams like this; I have.

We three riders were all fairly miserable and so each of us kind of went at our own fastest pace, trying to get some-where, anywhere, so we could get out of the weather. Towns are infrequent in northern New Mexico. Thirty-five miles up the road, what seemed to take an eternity, we ar-rived one by one at the almost *nonexistent* town of Glad-stone. I got there about an hour and a half after Bill and about a half hour after Kriss. I really can't exaggerate about how much slower I am in comparison to them. A lot! They were already well on their way to being warm and dry when I walked in to the Gladstone Mercantile Exchange, which was run by a kindly woman named Thelma.

When Bob Dylan wrote the line, "'Come in' she said, 'and I'll give you shelter from the storm,'" I think he must have had

Thelma at the Gladstone Mercantile in mind. She had plenty of hot coffee in a pot on the woodstove and we were welcome to it. She did not mind that we were walking around in our soggy, stocking feet, leaving wet footprints everywhere. She didn't even mind that we had strewn our wet clothing all over her store, so they might dry. She exuded a, "do what you need to do and don't worry about it," attitude. So we did.

I was sore, and wet, and cold, and grouchy and hungry. After a few minutes, I walked over to where Thelma was hanging out and asked if I could get a couple of eggs over easy with some whole wheat toast.

"Sure," she said. "But you should know that, even though we call it *whole wheat*, it really isn't. Is that okay?"

I nodded.

"You want some jelly with that?"

"Do you have strawberry?" I asked.

"No," she said. "But I do have some really good, homemade chokecherry jelly that I think you might like."

"Yep," I said, "sounds great." My meal was perfectly fine and certainly hit the spot. A little later, when we'd finally thawed out and dried up as much as we were going to, and it was time to start riding again, I asked Thelma what I owed her for my meal.

"Well," she said, "we don't really serve breakfast here. But I could see that you needed it. Do you think $2.50 would be okay?"

We were warmed not only by the woodstove at Thelma's Gladstone Mercantile Exchange, but also by the warmth of her gracious hospitality and generous care. I don't know how many times we said, "Thank you." It was quite a few.

When we got back outside, we looked up to the sky to see if there was any clearing in the weather. It looked just exactly as it had when we'd first stopped at Thelma's – foggy, drizzling, windy and cold. The sky and the horizon were indistinguishable through the rain, and it was still so foggy you couldn't see the fence posts along the side of the road. You could hear birds singing while roosting on the fence just a few feet away, but you couldn't see them. It may not have been any colder, but it wasn't any warmer either. Oh, well...

The thing was though, that now I was warm. I didn't feel cold again that whole day. Talk about a breakfast that sticks to your ribs!

"I've always depended on the kindness of strangers," said Blanche DuBois in "A Streetcar Named Desire." She's not alone in that regard. But I suppose that was Tennessee Williams' point. She wasn't alone. She depended on others. None of us are in this alone. We all depend on the kindness of strangers.

And in turn we have our moment in time of being the stranger, when it's time for us to be doing the giving. "All my life's a circle," Harry Chapin used to sing. I imagine that means we should take every opportunity, as Thelma did, to care for strangers ourselves. It's all goin' around and comin' around. Today you're at home and tomorrow you're the one that's on the road.

Moving on...

A funny thing happened a few more miles up the road from Thelma's Mercantile that same afternoon. A rancher drove past me. He got a little ways up the road and then his brake lights went on. Then he backed up and hopped out of his pick-up truck. "I'd be real glad to give you a ride into Clayton," he said.

"No thanks," said I. "That's my goal for the day. I'll have a couple of friends waiting for me when I get there." And then I told him a bit about our bike trip.

He pleaded with me, "It's terrible out here! What if one of these truck drivers *don't* see you in all this fog?"

"I'll be fine," I thanked him. I had a very bright red flashing light on the back of my bike. Every vehicle that had passed me all day had left a nice wide margin of safety as they'd gone around me. I knew I was visible. "I'll be fine," I said again. "And thank you so much for taking the time to stop and offering me a ride."

"Oh, don't mention it," he said. "And please forgive me for bargin' in on yer affairs like this." Can you imagine?! The one thing that might be worse than failing to extend hospitality for this fellow was the possibility of sticking his nose into somebody else's business.

It's as though, on this day – that had begun so miserably – I had stepped into a mirror image of the metaphor offered by the ancient Greek poet Homer, "The gods, likening themselves to all kinds of strangers, go in various disguises from city to city, observing the wrongdoing and the righteousness of [people]." Maybe this rancher was one of those gods? I don't know, but I did keep running into strangers who were like I imagine the gods throughout that entire experience.

Do you ever wonder if sometimes gods like to wait around until things get pretty bleak before they're willing to show themselves, even in disguise? Nah, there are too many times when things aren't bad at all and then something wonderful happens anyway.

My hope is that we all get to take turns at being the well-met stranger, and then at being the welcoming host. Hospitality is such a precious gift... from every perspective of it.

When I hear the media instructing parents of young children to teach their kids, "...never trust a stranger," it breaks my heart. We are saved through strangers; I'm sure of it. I don't think we can ever be saved, ever be sustained in isolation. We are part of an interdependent web of being. We are only saved, sustained, when we take others into consideration, and they do the same for us. I would hope we could teach our children to revere the stranger.

Moving on...

"[The Tao] has no beginning; even when followed it has no end."   -- Lao Tzu,

I'm not at all sure when this next story begins, or if it even has a beginning. So, I'll pick it up the week I graduated from high school, back in June of 1968. On that Saturday morning I accompanied my sister to the local Firestone Store where she was to get a new set of tires. She would pay for two of them; my brother and I, with whom she regularly and generously shared her very smart, little red and white Plymouth Valiant convertible, each paid for one of the two remaining tires. It only seemed fair.

I was looking for a summer job at the time and it occurred to me, while we waited on the installation, to ask for a job application. I filled it out and gave it to the salesman who had waited on us. Maybe five minutes later the store manager came around, introduced himself to me, and asked if I was serious about wanting a job. "Sure," I said.

"What do you know about changing tires?" he asked.

"Absolutely nothing," I answered.

"Why do you think I should consider you for a job?" he asked.

"Well, I was a wrestler for four years in high school," I said. "If I could do that, I imagine I'd do alright wrestling with tires, too."

"A wrestler," he repeated. "I used to wrestle in high school myself! Can you start work on Monday?"

"Sure can," I said. The following Monday morning I became a tireman.

I ended up working at that Firestone Store through the summer of '68, and then continued part time through my first two years of college. Try as I might to do otherwise, over the next decade and a half – off and on – I continued to be a tireman. Intermittently I was a college student, a Hospital Corpsmen in the U.S. Naval Reserve, was discharged as a Conscientious Objector and did my alternative service as a counselor in a residential psychiatric treatment center for adolescent boys for the Jewish Children's Bureau in Chicago. I was a student again and then a social worker for the Jane Addams Hull House Center in Uptown Chicago. I was an itinerant folk singer in the Midwest and then spent a year touring and singing in Europe. I got married as a very young man and divorced very soon after. I got married again, for real this time, and became a stay-at-home dad with our three children through their preschool years.

It wasn't so much that I sought it out, but in between several of these episodes I would find myself falling back on the reliability of employment as a tireman. In all, I worked in five different tire shops. Over the years, I moved up the tireman chain of expertise – beginning with passenger car tires, then truck tires and finally farm and large equipment tires. My last few years in the tire trade I owned and operated my own farm tire business, which was set in very rural Joe Daviess County, Illinois.

Area Tire Service lasted only a few years and ended as the result of a serious knee injury that led to surgery and the eventual sale of the business. I then returned to school once more, took only a few more minor detours, and emerged several years later as a Unitarian Universalist minister, which has been my trade for over the past two decades. During this more recent era, as you might imagine, I haven't had much need for my former identity as a tireman.

So as I rode my bike across the country, I found it rather surprising that on our very first day out we had two flat tires. On the second day we had another. By the time we reached the Delaware shore, we had accumulated over 40 flat tires. I was the resident tireman once more! Try as I might to flee that identity through the years, once again it had found me… or I had found it. Because I was the fastest and because we didn't want to lose any more time than necessary, I changed most of the tires myself and assisted in a few of the others so that Bill and Kriss could get some experience at it, too.

Here's a surprising thing about it though. It wasn't at all unpleasant. In fact, it was quite satisfying, even enjoyable. It provided a very agreeable break in our long, challenging days of pedaling. Most often, it created a space for easy conversation about any number of things. And it allowed this old tireman to feel that I was adding something of considerable value on a trip I was taking with two bikers whose athletic abilities were far superior to my own.

Changing tires is a lot more agreeable, at least for me, than one might guess. It's very physical, where the work of ministry is not. In ministry one rarely knows the outcome of their labors. With tires it's right there: there is a mechanical problem. There is a way of taking hold of that problem, applying a solution, and successfully moving things along from a state of brokenness to a state of wholeness. There are no questions left in the balance; at least usually there aren't.

I don't know why, but I've always been a sucker for geometry. I love it. It's like Euclid and I are soul brothers! Changing tires is all about applied geometry. There are circles, arcs, lines, areas, angles, and distributions of balance. Throw in a few challenging enigmas and changing tires is very much a geometrician's field day.

To top that off, changing tires – especially on large equipment or on bicycles – is almost always done out-of-doors. I love to be outside and I appreciate activities that take me there. The bicycle had trip provided me with a very agreeable opportunity to engage in a much loved ministry from my past – changing tires! Who'd have guessed?

Sometimes our lives seem to be lived out in segments, almost independent, one phase distinct from the next. Now we are students; now we are workers or professionals; now we are single; now we are partnered; now, sometimes, we are single again; now we are employed; now we are not; now we are injured or sick; now we are well; now we are youthful; now we are old. You can fill in your own segments. Round and round they roll.

So often in our work-a-day world, in our keep-busy-at-any-cost culture, we stay focused on the task at hand, and if at all on who we are merely in relation to that task or challenge. It's good from time to time, through sabbatical or even Sabbath, to take the time to remember the many facets of who we are on this grand journey of life. It's good to find our identity, beyond our experiences, as part of a larger whole, however difficult, however lonely, or grief-filled, or mundane, or even however wonderful our experiences might be.

Flat tires need to be and can be repaired. Our lives, too, often need to be and can be mended. The world can be made more whole. The relationships that allow us to be wounded healers are there for us to find. The connections are there for us to hold, and of course, to repair as needed.

Moving on...

It was yet another gray and overcast morning on the Kansas prairie; there had already been a few of them. We rode in and out of headwinds that weren't actually menacing; they were just a nuisance. Light rain fell intermittently. My riding companions and I were not soaked to the bone or freezing or anything like that, as we had been on a number of earlier occasions – Julian, California and Gladstone, New Mexico come to mind. But we were wet and not so terribly thrilled with the weather. So we stopped for a cup of coffee at a gas station in Mullinsville.

The local gas station in much of rural America has rather taken the place of the general store or the town café of yesteryear. It's a meeting place where local folks get together, out of the weather, to sip on coffee and mostly to visit with one another. Very often the same cast of characters can be found there at about the same time almost any given day, often sitting at the same seats of the same table. There's a kind of ritual to the gathering; the familiarity and constancy of the occasion is relaxed, and I imagine it provides comfort during trying times.

Even the casual visitor can recognize that there is a special table, a sacred spot that's meant for someone else. But the gas station in Mullinsville had only one table, and we needed a place to sit. There must have been a lull in the scheduled gathering for that particular hour. The table, which probably seated as many as 12 people, only had a couple of folks sitting at it and they didn't seem to mind a few interlopers.

So there we were, sitting at the table, sipping coffee, talking with each other and occasionally with one of the local women who was there waiting to meet with some friends. She was middle-aged, probably a bit younger and closer to the early end of middle-aged then we were. She seemed to be more of a town person than someone in from the farm. Her clothes weren't chore clothes. I happened to mention that we really had no idea of where we were. "You're about 10 miles west of Greensburg, Kansas," she said.

"Greensburg, Kansas," I repeated. It had a familiar ring. "Isn't that where a horrible tornado went through a while back, just about destroying everything in the town?"

"Yeah," she said. "I used to live in Greensburg. I grew up there but I've been here in Mullinsville for a good while now. I haven't even been able to bring myself to going back to Greensburg ever since the storm. They've been doing a really good job with things over there, though. They're rebuilding that town. They're making it all ecological and green and everything."

"Wow," I said. "I didn't even know we'd be going through Greensburg!" I knew about that cyclone and how it had leveled the town. I told her that, shortly after it had happened, I'd used a story that I'd heard about the storm as a sermon illustration. There was a woman who had lost her wedding ring and her mother's wedding ring when her family's house literally blew away. They had then found those rings a few days later. "It was an amazing story," I told her.

"Yeah, I think I heard about that too," she said. I imagined that she had. I'd heard it on National Public Radio's Morning Edition. I would think much of the country had heard that story.

It's not often that you connect with a story from halfway

across the continent, someplace you've never been, and use it as an illustration to encourage others in their practice of gratitude and their capacity to hope. And then, months later, as your life unfolds on a bicycle trip across the country, you find yourself a few minutes away from that same place where the story occurred. At least that sort of thing doesn't often happen to me!

By then the rain had stopped. We got back on our bikes. And then – in the blink of an eye – we were in Greensburg, Kansas. As it turned out, it just happened to be the exact weekend of the second anniversary of that tornado.

Wikipedia defines the word synchronicity as, "...the experience of two or more events which are causally unrelated occurring together in a meaningful manner. In order to count as synchronicity, the events should be unlikely to occur together by chance." I would add that a similar definition might be applied to the word, Grace. For me, this was a grace filled, synchronistic moment.

Moving on... But not moving on too far...

And so on Saturday, May 2nd our 20th day of the ride, we rode into Greensburg, Kansas. When we reached the western edge of town, you could see plenty of construction where brand new businesses, a gleaming new high school and homes still smelling of fresh-cut lumber now stood. Still-bulldozed sites, where you could see the locations of where other businesses, schools and homes had once stood, contrasted all of this. We got off of our bikes and stood on a huge cement slab that had once been the parking lot and the floor of a gas station. We observed with amazement the differences between the remnants of what had been and the affirmation of what was now beginning.

There weren't a lot of folks out on the edge of town, so after a bit, we rode in a bit further. As we got nearer to the center, we found ourselves amidst the hubbub of the two-year commemoration of the tornado. We went to the "Greensburg Green Town Center," where we met all kinds of people whose work was to bring new life into the town. There was a volunteer staff of housewives, college students and other environmentalists, who were there to tell the story of what Greensburg was becoming as it reinvented and recreated itself. There were townspeople there to see what was going on and groups of visitors from other towns and states.

Even though the primary focus was clearly on the future, we heard all kinds of stories about the storm, about the aftermath, and about the revitalization efforts that had been ongoing since then. The energy of the town and its people was palpable to anyone passing through, certainly to me.

Each time we met someone new from Greensburg, I'd ask about the woman who had lost and found the rings that I'd talked about in my sermon. I couldn't remember the name of the family or many of the exact details. What I could re-member was that the rings had been lost and then they'd been found, and that, at the heart of the story, there had been this relentless feeling and expression of gratitude and hope. I figured, small town, who knows? Maybe someone would know the family I was talking about.

I met a young man who was doing a college internship from a school in Louisiana who worked at the Town Center. It seemed ironic that this kid was a survivor of Hurricane Katrina and now he was in Kansas working on restoring this other storm torn town. I asked him about the rings. "I wasn't here when it happened," he said. "I did hear a story about it, though. And maybe I heard a couple of others a lot like it." But he couldn't remember any names specifically, either.

In passing, we were told about the newly rebuilt John Deere dealership where they were, that very day, commemorating the second anniversary of the storm along with their grand reopening. "It's a free barbecue lunch with all kinds of mu-sic and stuff going on." Someone suggested, "You should stop by, have something to eat and meet a bunch of the good folks who'll be there."

We hopped on our bikes and rode to the huge new dealer-ship at the edge of town. There was a massive new struc-ture where the gathering of as many as 1,500 people from Greensburg and the outlying areas, *if an outlying area can have outlying areas*, had answered the invitation to come and celebrate the recovery and the opening over a barbecue lunch with entertainment. There must have been close to 200 hundred tables that each seated up to ten people and they were mostly filled with people eating, talking and lis-tening to the Barbershop Gospel Quartet that was perform-ing on a makeshift stage.

Within a few minutes, Bill and I were in the food line, heading toward – *what looked like and later proved to be* – a totally excellent barbecue dinner. (I loved being back in my part of the world where the noon meal is called *dinner!*) We did meet lots of good folks in line. And each time we met someone new, I'd mention the story about the woman and the rings. No luck.

A short while later, with our plates filled to overflowing, we found space to sit at a long table along with three generations of a family that was clearly headed by its matriarch in residence, Jolene. She and her husband, Max, invited us to join them and then welcomed us like we were part of the family. You might want to remember just how Bill and I, and by this point we'd been rejoined by Kriss, how we must have looked to our hosts and this room full of very rural Midwesterners. We were there in our brightly colored biking shirts and our spandex shorts that looked like they might have been spray-painted on. To top that off, I was wearing a headband fashioned from a bandanna, in order to keep my hair out of my eyes!
Just the same, Jolene, Max and family took us in like we were their own.

We talked a bit about the bike trip and we talked a lot about the storm – where they had been, how they got through it, how their home did not. We talked about how they had put their lives back together, about how much they appreciated one another... and of course, about how grateful they were. Jolene loved to laugh and there was lots of laughter among all of us at that table. It was wonderful.

When I got around to asking if any of them knew the family from the story about the rings, Jolene said, "Well sure, that's Steve Burke you're talking about. Oh look," she smiled. "There's Steve now." She pointed to a guy carrying a plate of food just a few feet away. Jolene jumped up, ran over to Steve, took him by the arm, and, I imagine, gave him some kind of an explanation of her table guests. She brought him over to the table and sat him down, right across from me. "This is your guy," she said. "This is Steve Burke and it was his wife's and her mother's wedding rings that got lost."

So I got to sit and have lunch with Steve for about the next half hour. He told me the story of how their house had been leveled and how the rings had been lost; how, days later, their teenaged son had found one of the rings, and then how the two of them had searched the same area until the other one was found. He told me about how he swore his son to secrecy and about how that night at supper he'd asked his wife to close her eyes and to hold out her hand. And then he told me that while he slipped the wedding ring back on her finger, he'd said, "With this ring, I thee wed.

Oh, Charlie," he said. "She just started crying. You wouldn't believe it!"

"Steve," I said, blowing my nose into my napkin and wiping my eyes, "I can't stop crying just hearing about it."

He was moved to learn that I'd used the story in a sermon back in Montclair, and that it had touched a number of the folks there. Jolene and Max and everyone rejoined the con-versation as I shared with them how their story, the story of Greensburg, had played out in the press, especially on Na-tional Public Radio. "What came through most clearly," I said, "was your undying sense of hope and how it seemed to be based in your ability to experience gratitude even during such an unbelievable time of loss."

"We're so glad that's what people heard," they all agreed. And that's when Steve Burke's eyes began to well up with tears. "You can't imagine what it was like to have lost everything that you owned," he said. "It's just gone and you're devastated. You think about those poor folks down in New Orleans, who were abandoned; you have to feel for them. But after our storm all kinds of folks came to town – to help out and to hear us tell our stories. And it was so clear that they cared. And then you can't help but to feel, deep in your heart, so very grateful. You've got nothing, and still people care. That's something to be grateful about...and it gives you hope."

It wouldn't have mattered to me if we'd left Greensburg and came straight home that same afternoon. The trip had been made for me – wholly and holy – sitting there at that table, basking in the riches that had been laid out before me. It was a very precious gift.

Probably less than 2 ½ hours after we'd leaned them up against the new sign in the front of the dealership, we got back on our bikes. We started pedaling east towards Pratt, our destination for the day. It was about another 40 miles up the road.

20th Century Renaissance person Albert Schweitzer once commented on gratitude: "To educate yourself for the feeling of gratitude means to take nothing for granted, but to always seek out and value the kind that will stand behind the action. Nothing that is done for you is a matter of course. Everything originates in a will for the good, which is directed at you. Train yourself never to put off the word or action for the expression of gratitude."

The truth is that the storm in Greensburg did not really destroy most everything that was there. There was a lot of destruction; it's true. But a good many jewels were un-earthed by that storm as well. Taking nothing for granted, the good people of Greensburg took stock. In that they found good reason for gratitude. And in their gratitude they found good reason for hope.

Moving on... But still not moving much further...

Greensburg really was one of the richer fields for mining metaphors. Everyone was invited to the Grand Reopening of the John Deere Dealership, we'd been told. "You all are invited, too," we were assured by folks in town. "Go on out there and have yourselves some lunch," they said. "You'll meet lots of nice folks out there, too." And we did. At one point I was introduced to Mrs. Kelly Estes, the wife of the couple that owned the dealership. Mrs. Estes assured me that we were indeed welcome and that she was only too pleased that we could see for ourselves, her town of Greensburg at its best. She encouraged us to eat our fill, "...and then some!"

The lines to the several dozen tables serving the down-home and delicious cooking were formidable but they moved along at a good clip. The time spent on line provided a great chance to meet and visit with a good many people along the way. Kriss, who is something of an introvert, had wandered off on his own for a while. Bill and I, both off-the-chart extroverts on the Myers/Briggs Personality Scale, had a great time meeting and chatting with people as we snaked our way along with and through the masses that were there to celebrate.

I mentioned earlier that we sort of stuck out in the crowd because of our biking outfits and what appeared to be our sprayed-on Lycra biking shorts. No one seemed to think of us as strange, though. At least they did a good job of not appearing like they thought of us as strange. I'm somewhat chagrinned that, at least in my head, I couldn't help but noticing a few dozen folks there, scattered through the crowd, who had a very Amish-like appearance. One of those couples was just in front of us in the food line.

They were Kent and Ann Brewbaker. Kent wore a straw hat and trousers held up by suspenders. The sleeves of his broad cloth shirt were rolled up; he sported a clean upper lip and a long beard that was allowed to grow only from the under regions of his square chin. Ann wore a long cotton dress. Her hair was done up in a bun that was covered by a white lace cap that tied under her chin. She also wore the ultimate in sensible walking shoes, which laced up over the tops of her ankles and were constructed of sturdy black leather.

I don't know about you, but I have to admit to often having had a little discomfort around folks who look like Kent and Ann. I have found them to be a bit standoffish, which has been fine by me, because I've never really known what I might say to start a conversation. They tend to be on the very conservative end of the religious spectrum and I... well, I don't. But the thing is, I'm the one who has really missed the boat!

Turns out, Kent and Ann were not Amish anyway. They were members of the Ana Baptist Church of the German Brethren. They didn't live in Greensburg but about 25 miles away in the town of Sawyer. They had a big farm and did a lot of business with the Estes' John Deere Dealership. And they didn't come to town in a horse and carriage, but drove a Ford pickup, their usual mode of transportation.

Kent had a peculiar sense of humor, much like my own. And so the four of us quite enjoyed our visit on the way to the serving tables. There was a lot of joking around and a whole lot of laughter. I have to wonder though, if the Brewbakers had to dispel reservations and biases about us because of our appearance, too. No matter, we quickly became good friends as can only happen when people meet on the road. There, you make friends fast or not at all.

By the time we got served and our plates were loaded, we'd somehow managed to go in a different direction from the Brewbakers. When Bill and I found a place to sit we couldn't find Kent and Ann. About an hour later though, they found us. They were getting ready to leave and wanted to say goodbye (maybe our attire made it easier for them to pick us out of the crowd??!!). We'd talked a bit about our bike trip in our earlier conversation in the food line, but the Brewbakers wanted to know more about it.

We told them about our daily rituals and typical distances we would try to manage in a day. We talked about our route and some of the things we'd seen. And we talked about Toni's Kitchen and about raising money and awareness regarding hunger. They asked where we were hoping to get by the end of that day's ride. The conversation was about the kinds of things you'd talk about with friends that wanted to get to know one another better. Then a big flow of people came through and sort of washed Kent and Ann away in its current. "Goodbye, God bless..." they hollered as they disappeared into the crowd.

"Great people," Bill said.

"Yeah," I agreed. "Great people. I liked them."

About three hours and 32 miles down the road, we were nearing the town of Pratt, which was our destination for the day. As we went through the crossroads just before town, we came upon a pickup truck pulled over to the side of the road. The driver was honking and waving for us to come over. Sure enough, it was Kent and Ann Brewbaker. Somehow they figured out where we'd be and how long it would take us to get there. "We just wanted to make a little contribution to that soup kitchen," Kent said, slipping me a couple of $20 bills.

"And we want to invite you to join us at a community pot-luck dinner tonight in Sawyer," Ann said. "It's potluck, but we'll be bringing plenty enough to cover for all of us. It's only 10 miles straight south of Pratt. It'll be at the firehouse and it starts at 6:30. You can drive your RV down there. Sure hope you can join us."

By 6:30 we'd shaved, showered and shined ourselves up, and we were walking into the firehouse in Sawyer, Kansas. We were there for the community potluck dinner to raise funds for a new truck for the volunteer fire department. About half of the folks there were from the Ana Baptist Church of the German Brethren; the other half was not. We were friends of the Brewbakers though, so we got to sit with the Ana Baptist crowd. We ate and talked and laughed a lot. Theological discourse was quite unnecessary. By the way, the food was about as good as it gets. So was our experience with our new friends.

Novelist and poet, Charlotte Bronte wrote, "Prejudices, it is well known, are most difficult to eradicate from the heart whose soil has never been loosed or fertilized by education; they grow there, firm as weeds among rocks."

I'm not saying that I would make as good of friends with all members of the Ana Baptist Church of the German Brethren as I became with the Brewbakers. Then again, I couldn't say that I wouldn't. In relation to Charlotte Bronte's thought about the need for education to eradicate prejudice, I don't think there's any education quite as profound as experience, and there's no better classroom than a table spread with good food and surrounded by good folks. That is to say, we learn about people by being with them. We are trans-formed by being in relationships with others.

Moving on...

It was an exquisite Sunday morning in Kansas. We had just spent what seemed like forever crossing this state in a 1984-ish gray mist that had for days refused to relent. But finally spring had returned; the morning was gorgeous! The sun had reclaimed its dominance of the sky; the buds and blossoms in the gardens we passed blushed with ardor in their newly added luster. The sumptuous morning air was warm enough to ride in a light jacket. We were feeling... p-r-e-t-t-y good.

Bill had hung behind in town to do some work on his trip blog. Kriss and I had set out to begin the day's ride. We were taken by the rural Kansas landscape, which is as flat as it's renowned to be, but punctuated about every 10 miles by a grain elevator rising up like a beacon in each passing town. We were enveloped by the zest of the season that permeated the air.

Kriss and I talked as we rode along. We talked about the clarity of the morning and about the trip up to this point. Things had started out a little rough, but now problems with my equipment and our physical conditioning had been resolved. The excruciating mountain climbs that had challenged us in the beginning were well behind us now. The foul weather that had been with us for the past several days had finally redeemed itself, at least for a while. Who knew? We might even get out of Kansas and into Missouri within another day or so. We were enjoying ourselves and each other and the feeling of resurgence on this early morning ride on a perfectly lovely day.

We were rolling along at a decent clip of about 20 mph and we'd been chatting for a while. Long conversations come easily to me; I happen to be an off-the-chart extrovert. But Kriss is as much an introvert as I am the opposite. He needs occasional rest periods from conversation. I can appreciate that sort of thing, even if I don't understand it. So, after a while he pulled a few yards ahead of me for some downtime and we continued on our way, enjoying the day and the sparingly elegant Kansas countryside.

As we neared the little town of Cunningham, there were some railroad tracks that ran along the opposite side of the road we were traveling on, U.S. Highway 51. We'd been riding parallel to them for several miles, but looking ahead, I could see the lines crossing over the road a ways up ahead of me. What I couldn't see though, was the angle at which they crossed.

The safest way to cross railroad tracks on a bicycle is to take them at a 90° angle. I could see that Kriss had crossed them just fine, so I anticipated that I wouldn't have any problems either. When I got to the tracks though, I found that they actually ran just along the edge of the road for a stretch, at a very slight angle, something like the flattened ends of a bell curve, before they got all the way over off of the road.

For me to cross over the tracks at a right angle would have required darting straight out onto the highway. Because I hadn't adequately anticipated the situation, it was too late to look back and see if there was any traffic coming up from behind me. In an instant I was going to be forced to cross the tracks at a very acute angle. By then I had no choice; I held on tight and went for it.

I don't know how it works for you, but often when I'm in precarious situations and start to fall, things... seem... to... go... in... very... slow... motion. I experience having plenty of time to size up my situation and every opportunity to go for the best option available. But this time was a little different. At 20 mph things didn't seem to have a chance to slow down quite enough.

I remember having three thoughts as my fall unfolded. The first thought occurred as I experienced abandonment from my sense of balance. As my front tire slipped into the implacable groove between the rail and the road, I analytically perceived, "I'm going down!"

The next thought struck as I felt my helmet slap against the pavement, literally bouncing off of it. I actually felt the pressure of the blow dissipate around the left hemisphere of my head as the helmet absorbed the concussion and saved my skull. I gratefully observed, "Helmet worked!"

The final thought in this series came as I found myself lying out in the middle of the road. My legs were tangled up in the frame of the bike so badly that I couldn't begin free myself; I wasn't even sure if I could move. I wearily submitted my will to this newly emerging reality. "Oh, shit," were the words that were attached to the thought that passed through my mind.

My front wheel was pretty bent up and jammed in the fork. But before the rear tire stopped spinning Kriss had raced back to my side. The very first car that came by stopped and the driver got out to help Kriss help me. They slowly untangled me from the bike and eventually helped me to my feet. Lots of other cars would stop in the next several minutes, all of the drivers checking to see if they could help in any way.

I was in something of a stupor for a while, so I'm not sure just what the timing of what followed might have been. To say that I was moving slowly would be to overstate my movement altogether. I was dazed. I immediately knew that my world had changed. I didn't have a clue to what extent. My hope was that it wouldn't be all that much, but it felt very odd not knowing.

I had a puncture wound in my right thigh. A full-length patch of road rash – tiny grains of gravel included – covered the outside of my left shin. The pain that I was beginning to feel in my left thigh would eventually produce a massive bruise that entertained us with changing colors for the next several weeks. The worst injury seemed to be to my left shoulder; I wasn't able to move my left arm at all.

Martha, Kriss's wife who was Tiggie's driver during that stretch of the trip, arrived with the RV a short while later. It wasn't much longer before Bill got there on his bike. My own bicycle was as un-ride-able as I was unfit to ride it. We all agreed that I needed to get to the nearest emergency room to be examined and cleaned up. Kriss and Bill would continue along on their bikes. Martha and I would set in out in Tiggie for the hospital 15 miles away. The guys would meet up with us there. Ah, but the saga continues...

Martha and I got no further than about two or three miles up the road when we heard a loud bang and Tiggie began to convulse wildly. Somehow we had blown out both dual tires on the left rear of the RV! Martha managed safely to pull over to the shoulder of the road, which was quite an accomplishment by the way, one that took a great deal of strength and determination on her part.

Tireman or not, I was in no condition to get out of Tiggie to investigate the situation. Martha, remaining quite composed, got out and started walking back along the road to find the nearest mile marker. She wanted to be ready to identify our location when she called the road service company. Turned out, as had happened earlier, the very first vehicle to come along stopped.

The driver, a man in his early 40's whose name was Tom, asked if there was anything he might do to be helpful. Martha explained what had happened to me and then what happened to the RV. She told Tom that we were en route to the ER at the hospital in Kingman when the tires blew. Through the open window I heard her ask, "Do you think you might be able get this man to the hospital?"

"Sure can," Tom said in less than a flash. A few minutes later he and I were tooling along U.S. Highway 51 on our way to Kingman. He'd been on his way to mow the lawn at his widowed mother's house, which she had recently moved from to enter a nursing home. Her house, of course, happened to be in the opposite direction from the hospital where we were heading. It was, "...no big deal at all," to take a 20-mile round-trip that was completely out of his way in order to get me to the ER.

When we got there, Tom pulled up to the door, walked me inside and stayed with me until, just a few minutes later, I was taken into an examination cubicle. Then he went back out to re-park his car in a legal spot in the hospital a lot. Next he came back into the examination room to make sure that I was receiving the kind of treatment he would expect for himself. Only after he was sure that I was being well cared for did Tom leave me at the hospital and head out for his date with his mother's lawn.

Good news. The report from the emergency room x-ray technician was that I had no broken bones. As she wheeled me back to the examination room, she confided, "It's odd, you know. I did an x-ray last year on a guy who fell on those same railroad tracks, at that exact same spot. You'd think somebody might do something about that!" I felt perversely gratified by the information; misery does always love company.

Back in my cubicle, the nurse kindly anesthetized my road rash wounds so that she'd be able to clean them out without having to listen to me scream. That was a good thing. When I was released, they gave me some pills for the pain, which they assured me would be worse the next day. They all wished me well and suggested that I take it easy for a while. "No bike riding for two or three days, at least." They were adamant.

The morning after, I still was unable to move my left arm. Bill and I tried to think of what kind of medical advice services might be available by phone for people who ran into trouble while they were on the road. After a while, it occurred to me (duh!) I didn't have to locate someone I didn't know for advice. I phoned my physical therapist back home in Montclair. Todd, who had gotten me through other difficult times in the past, gave me a long-distance diagnostic assessment and assured me that there was no way he could be certain of just what my injuries might be. But then he went on to suggest a regimen of exercises that he hoped would be helpful in getting my shoulder to loosen up.

Later that same morning, after Kriss and Bill had set out on their bikes, Martha and I took my bike to The Tom Sawyer Bike Shop in Wichita. Their ad in the Yellow Pages, "Your Family-Friendly Bicycle Shop Since 1963," seemed particularly inviting. Alan Keimig was the owner of Tom Sawyer. His family, I learned, had come from the same small town in Germany as mine. We might have even been related! In Alan's hands, my bike got the same kind of expert and caring treatment I had received the day before in the ER. "Let's call it even at $18," Alan said after working on it for about two hours.

By Tuesday I was able to get on my bike, clip my shoes to the petals and ride for six miles – the last three miles of Kansas and the first three miles of Missouri! By the third day, Wednesday, I was back on the ride with Bill and Kriss for a full 60-mile day. It was so excellent to be back in the saddle again!

I said before that I knew my world had changed but didn't know how or how much. Fortunately, the lasting physical impact was minor. I now have a scar in the shape of Illinois (my home state!) left over from the road rash on the outside of my left shin. I'm also a bit more accurate these days in predicting impending rainstorms, from the alert that emanates from my left shoulder before they occur. I came though it all rather well, I'd say.

Still, the experience of the fall was both life threatening and life giving as it unfolded. Of the myriad lessons that might be drawn from it, there are three that I take most to heart:

Ω   Railroad crossings or other obstacles of unknown character or quality, which lie in the paths of our lives, need to be taken seriously. They don't have to be deal stoppers, but awareness of them can provide excellent guideposts in helping us to go forward safely. And just because somebody else does something doesn't mean that I have to!

Ω   We are our brothers' and sisters' keepers. The story of the Good Samaritan isn't just a nice story with a kindly moral. It's a story, confirmed by this experience that provides a map for sustainability. We are upheld and nurtured in this world by our valuable interactions with others, especially including the stranger. We are sustained and sustaining to others when all of us reach back and forth, beyond our personal boundaries, making sure that everyone's needs are being met.

Ω	The use of bicycle helmets saves lives. I would be dead, dead, dead, if I hadn't been wearing a helmet. I am alive now only because I was wearing one then. I want everyone to know that, and I want your children and your neighbors' children to know it too.

Postscript... One lesson that I refuse to take away from this adventure/misadventure is the thought that it's harmful or bad luck to talk about how well things are going. To talk about how good things are is to appreciate them. Appreciation is a form of gratitude. That's where I want to live, in a state of gratitude. Kansas on the other hand is another state. But this isn't Kansas anymore!

Moving on...

"As if whipped by invisible spirits, the sun steeds of time run away with the light chariot of our destiny, and nothing remains to us but to hold onto the reins with calm courage, steering the wheels, now right, now left, from the stone here and the abyss there. Where it goes—who knows? One hardly remembers from where one came."
                                        --Johann Wolfgang von Goethe

I want to share a couple of assumptions that I held at the onset of the trip, and how those assumptions played out in reality. For the first one, I suppose the metaphor is that of *order*. In an orderly universe, things unfold in an orderly manner, yes? Another name for this metaphor might be *the scientific method*. I actually do subscribe to this metaphor. Certain things give way to other things that one can trace back to some kind of origin.

Understanding what has happened helps us to predict what will or might occur. The point is though, that it's easy to get caught up in the idea that we can reach into the *great mystery* and grab hold of a handful of predictable orderliness. The order of things is so much easier to see in retrospect than it is when we're in the midst of unfolding things, like... say... a long bicycle trip.

One of my early assumptions was that it would be smart to plan the trip so that we'd be riding with a tailwind most of the time, by traveling from the west coast to the east coast. It made good sense. Whenever you listen to the weather forecast on any given day, you hear about weather patterns moving from the west to the east. It's that way all the way across the continent, right?

Riding over 3,000 miles pushed merrily along by prevailing

tailwinds, seemed to make a lot more sense than going the opposite direction, which one would think would have us riding into headwinds. That was the assumption. The reality of our experience though, proved that there is no such thing as a prevailing tailwind. Oddly enough, the reverse situation, prevailing headwinds, do indeed exist. Prevailing headwinds are not only a reality, they are...well...they are prevailing. Our trip lasted 46 days; we actually rode on 44 of those days. On at least 40 of the riding days, we pedaled directly into headwinds that ranged in velocity from a mild breeze to 40 mph *or so*. Riding as fast as you can into a 40 mph wind sort of takes your breath away and it sometimes leaves you going barely fast enough to stay upright. At least that's what it did to me!

Goethe wrote, "As if whipped by invisible spirits, the sun steeds of time run away with the light chariot of our destiny..." I'm pretty sure he was talking about headwinds. And I know he was right; they did run away just like that. I don't understand how it worked, though. It's part of the great mystery I suppose.

I sometimes wondered if I turned around and headed into the opposite direction, if the winds would turn right around with me. Call me paranoid, but I suspected that if I did turn around, they would still be blowing right into my face. I suppose thoughts like that could be considered grandiose thinking. Imagining that nature will or ought to meet our expectations – even when our expectations are at odds with what we might want – is really some kind of grandiosity or at least arrogance.

How often do we feel that if, just something were or weren't so (whatever that something might be) that we would be better off and our lives would be so much more satisfying? I'm guessing that, if we spend a lot of time looking for something that isn't in our own back yards, it probably isn't something that we really need anyway (thank you, Dorothy!).

Latina mystic and author, Laura Teresa Marquez, warns that, "Arrogance and rudeness are training wheels on the bicycle of life – for weak people who cannot keep their balance without them."

Complaining about headwinds is probably a lot like crying over spilt milk. What's the use? My late father-in-law would often say, "You just have to play the hand you were dealt, Charlie." When we learn not to cry over spilt milk, or not to get stuck wanting other cards, dreading the hands we've been dealt *or the circumstances of our lives*, that's when we grow up and can take those training wheels off. The truth is, they really do slow us down way too much anyway, sort of like headwinds I suppose.

The other assumption I had early on was that this ride would provide endless hours, even days of uninterrupted time for contemplation of the universe. While, as I believe I've illustrated numerous times already, assumptions so often fail to pan out, this was one that really came true. I had hoped to ponder the universe in exploration of what for me would be uncharted territories of new discoveries, realizations and sensitivities. And that is exactly what I had plenty of time to do.

What I had not imagined though, was just exactly what part of the universe might be available for my scrutinization. Would I find myself considering the infinitely vast expanses of the macrocosmic heavens? Would I be absorbed in the immeasurably microscopic realm of the molecular underpinnings of existence? What I often think of as *divine* or as *the great mystery* can sometimes be approached from the macro or the micro levels, experienced in either a grand larger view of the cosmos where heavenly bodies dance in swirling, cyclical rhythm, or in an infinitesimally miniscule view of the atom's pulsating, undulating whirl of positive and negative ions.

What I got on the ride was somewhere in between. The part of the universe where I found my attention riveted was a particularly well-defined segment of it. What I saw was the ever constant and yet continually varying patch of road that lay just in front of me. My field of vision tended to be about 10 to 15 yards wide, by about 10 to 100 yards deep.

Still, that was the part of the universe within which I mostly found my being, in which I understood my experience. It was from there that I could appreciate a perspective of my past and anticipate the future. Within the field of that distinct rectangular but not impermeable enclosure, lay all the verities of my existence and – in truth – the answers to my deepest questions, on any given day. Within the limits of those parameters, I was able to find the world I lived in and it was in that world where I found myself.

At times it seemed that I was the only living thing within that space. But that was an illusion. My few hundred square feet of universe was loaded with life of all kinds. Flora, fauna, wildlife, not such wildlife, friends, strangers, machines and all kinds of things filled my universe at various times. I found myself there in relationship to and with all of them.

At least I was able to find myself there when I took the time and had the inclination to notice. The point is, whatever we perceive our limitations to be, however we might limit our perspectives, the point is... to pay attention. The point is to notice.

The challenge is to see through the illusion of our limits. That's sure a lot easier said than done. Still, I have to believe it is worth doing. It seems there is always so much more to notice and pay attention to.

The late Les Brown, longtime leader of "Les Brown and His Band of Renown," was something of a philosopher in his own right. He had a definitive view on the boundaries of human experience. He said, "Life has no limitations, except the ones you make." The Buddha also taught that there are never really any limits within our perceived or self-imposed restrictions. There is only the possibility for the refinement and the expansion of our perspective. I wonder if maybe he meant that it's the refinement of the macro, and the expansion of the micro levels of existence. At any rate, we are here, the Buddha taught, to pay attention and to notice.

Moving on...

I suspect that you may have also experienced that cell phones don't always work with the greatest consistency across much of this country. There were lots of places on the road where I wasn't able to get service at all. Eventually though, I would always manage to get messages, even if I couldn't speak directly to the person trying to reach me. Sometimes this made things seem cumbersome, but then I'd remember that it wasn't so many years ago that there were no cell phones at all. Funny how things, like our expectations, change but some things don't change very much at all.

I saw that I had a voicemail when I woke up on the morning of our 24th day; we were in Hermitage, Missouri. The call had come in sometime the night before. Someone from the church had phoned to say that Nancy Knoerzer, an 84-year-old member of the congregation, was dying. They didn't think she would live another 24 hours.

Nancy had been the president of the church when I first arrived in Montclair fourteen and a half years earlier. She had, at that time, just led the congregation through a very difficult interim ministry and was feeling a bit battered when I got there. She was not all that sure whether or not she was willing to just turn the place, *her place*, over to this new minister coming down from Massachusetts.

It really was *her place*. Nancy's parents had been members of the congregation. She had been a part of it and it had been a part of her for four score and four years, to lean on a phrase from history. And Nancy was the congregation's historian. She carried most of the 112 years of its history in her head as well as in her heart. She and I had struggled a lot that first year.

By the end of it though, our mutual love for and dedication to the congregation had transformed our personal relationship into one of considerable love and trust for one another. Over the years that relationship grew – through good times and bad, as they say. Together we buried her son, celebrated holidays and several of her birthdays. Along with my own children, I'd helped her plant seedling trees on her organic Christmas tree farm. Together we had both worried over and reflected happily on events in the lives of her children and grandchildren. Many times we'd shared concerns about her health issues. She had lots of health issues and they were enormously complicated by the addition of diabetes.

I had visited her many times in the hospital in the weeks immediately preceding the bike trip, a trip that she was excited about and had encouraged me to take. On those visits we laughed and cried, talked and sang together. I suspected when I saw her the day before I left for Carlsbad to begin the trip that it would be the last time I would see her alive. That was hard.

Now I was close to 1,500 miles away and Nancy was back home actively dying. I made an early morning call to her house. The cell phone cooperated. Stacey, her nurse-manager whom I'd come to know and appreciate, answered. "The girls (Nancy's daughters) have gone to Chris' to get a little rest," she said. "Nancy's had a really rough night, Charlie. It seems like she just can't let go."

Stacey and I talked for a bit and then I said, "Please tell her that I love her and that I'm praying that she'll be able to go easily."

I got off the phone and immediately wondered, "Why didn't

I tell her that myself?"

Throughout the morning I found myself pedaling along through the countryside singing the hymn, "For the Beauty of the Earth," Nancy's all-time favorite.

When we broke to eat lunch on a picnic table in front of an old, closed down and falling apart root beer stand on the side of the road, I called the house again. I expected to hear that she had died sometime during the morning. "She's still here," Nancy's oldest daughter, Lee, told me. "She won't let go, Charlie." Lee and I talked for a while more and then I asked Lee to put the phone up to Nancy's ear so that I could speak to her. I've been in the ministry business long enough to have learned that, even in a deep coma, people some-times hear what's said to them. Lee said she would. I was given a dispensation, a second chance to say goodbye for myself.

Lee put the phone to her mother's ear and I got to speak to Nancy for a couple of minutes. I didn't have to think of what to say; the words just flowed. I was able for a final time to say all of the things I would hope to say to this octogenarian whom I loved and admired and who had lived such a noble life filled with integrity.

Finally, Lee took the phone back and we said goodbye. It was a day later when I learned that Nancy died about ten minutes after our phone call had ended. I don't know that the two events were connected, though I think they might well have been. Anyway, she had finally let go...

We live in an unbelievable age of technology that can some-times be such an incredible blessing. I was more than half-way across the country and yet had been given the oppor-tunity to be present at the bedside of a dying loved one back in Montclair. Through the miracle of technology, I was actually able to be in two places at once. I was pedaling down the highways of Missouri through terrain I'd never seen before; at the same time I was connecting back home to a person and a set of ideals that have been a part of my life for a very long time. Amazing.

Relationships – that's how we know who we are. That's how others know us. It doesn't happen, and can't happen in a vacuum. It's always in relationships… with people, with ideas and values, with our planet.

Japanese Aikido sensei and philosopher, Mitsugi Saotome, put it this way:
"If you were all alone in the universe with no one to talk to, no one with which to share the beauty of the stars, to laugh with, to touch, what would be your purpose in life? It is other life, it is love, which gives your life meaning. This is harmony. We must discover the joy of each other, the joy of challenge, the joy of growth."

A lot of times I think that spirituality and spiritual practice is misunderstood when it is seen as a pious, individual en-deavor to withdraw one's self from the world. Some folks believe that this is the way to have a personal relationship with their idea of the divine. Nancy Knoerzer used to scorn such sentiment. It doesn't work so well for me either. I think spirituality is about paying attention to the connec-tions that bind each of us to all that is. If God is love, as we used to say in the 60s, then loving relationships provide a path that leads us towards interconnections and interde-pendence and maybe towards sustainability…for the beauty of the earth.

Maya Angelou wrote these words that I shared at Nancy's memorial service in June after my return home:

"And when great souls die, after a period peace blooms,
slowly and always irregularly:
Spaces fill with a kind of soothing electric vibration.
Our senses, restored, never to be the same,
whisper to us.
They existed. They existed.
We can be. Be and be better.
For they existed."

Moving on...

"I like nonsense. It wakes up the brain cells."   -- Dr. Seuss

We passed through Camdenton, Missouri on May 7th. Perhaps you've heard of Camdenton. It is the county seat of Camdenton County and it exists smack in the middle of the state. It is home to nearly 3,000 souls who lived there as full-time residents. More notably, Camdenton is nestled into the serpentine shoreline of the Lake of the Ozarks, which came into existence in 1931 by the completion of the Bagnell Dam on the Osage River. Some of the locals still debate over whether or not it was a good idea, but most of the folks there reap substantial benefits from it.

The population of Camdenton swells annually with the migration of tourists that begin to arrive with warmer weather. We rode into town on U.S. Highway 54 along with many of those tourists. They were eager to get a jump on the season and, no doubt, getting after the fish that had been waiting there to be caught since the end of last season.

It was cozy there on the highway, all those backed up cars pulling so close to each other and to us on our *unbumpered* bicycles. Many of the drivers tied up in that jam had obviously been in it for a long while. Some of them were there long enough to grow just a tad impatient and impulsive. Some of them developed an inexplicable urge to pull out of their lane without looking to see who else might be around. There were other less than optimal driving behaviors displayed as well. But that's hardly the most memorable thing that we took away with us from Camdenton.

There was road construction everywhere. It seemed to encompass the entire town. Even though it was a clear, warm spring day, the dust clouds kicked up by all the machinery actually blocked out much of the sunlight, casting an eerie shade, somewhat like a solar eclipse. The dust filled our eyes with grit to the point that we could hardly keep them open, especially while riding down some of the steeper grades in the area. But even the construction and the dust that went with it weren't the most memorable things about Camdenton.

What was most memorable was the signage that greeted us as we entered the town. It was designed as a collage containing three separate signs festooned to two signposts. It must have been imagined by a person of considerable thought, someone who enjoyed the randomness of this ironic universe. I loved it.

The two vertical posts were positioned parallel to each other. About two thirds of the way up from the ground, the posts were spanned by the lower and larger of the three signs. It formed a sort of crossbar like on a football goal-post. This horizontal sign between the two posts provided your traditional green, town border sign. It was printed on three lines. In small print the top line read, "CITY LIMITS." In larger, bolder letters the middle line read, "**CAMDEN-TON**." The bottom line, again in smaller print, proclaimed, "POP. 2779."

At the top of each upright, there was an additional rectangular sign, black lettering over a white background, indicating rules that any lawful visitor would surely want to obey while passing through Camdenton. One could not help but to read them both together at the same time.

The sign at the top of the left upright was quite prescriptive, "SPEED LIMIT 50 MPH." Clear enough! But it was the sign at the top of the right upright that brought everything into question making the two signs together precious. It read, "SPEED LIMIT 25 EXCEPT WHERE POSTED."

It was sort of like telling a child, "You can go out and play anytime you want. But not now!" You have to wonder if that might have been what got the motorists all teed off. At this point in time, there was nowhere in Camdenton where they could get up to 25 mph, let alone 50. For Bill, Kriss and me, the idea of going even 25 mph was always much more of an aspiration that it was a limit.

Humorist and author Don Williams, Jr. wrote of irony when he said (and I paraphrase here because I'd like to think this is a child-friendly book), "A mind is like a parachute. If it doesn't open you're screwed." It takes a brain that can think in at least two directions at once to appreciate irony. But isn't thinking in two directions at once also a definition of psychosis? Either way, the signs welcoming us to Camdenton also welcomed us to a little levity in the midst of a dusty, hilly, heavy traffic jam. There really is always so much to be thankful for...

Moving on...

What's not to love about a beautiful spring day? Once we had gotten beyond the upper elevations of the western mountain ranges, with a few notable exceptions, we pretty much followed some very primo spring weather across most of the country. It was warm, but not overly hot. The skies were mostly clear with just enough occasional cloud cover to keep the sun from being oppressive. Almost everywhere we rode, we passed through towns with beautiful gardens, blossoming fruit trees and bucolic neighborhoods of houses that were extended by expansive porches, complete with gliders or swings. To say that much of the spring and its weather provided us with a salubrious experience – immersion or envelopment in an environment of comfort, health and well-being – would hardly be hyperbole.

That's how the weather and our experience of it were on the 29th day of the trip, on May 11th. We couldn't have asked for a finer day to cross the Mississippi, the river of my childhood, and enter my home state of Illinois. We began the day in St. Charles, Missouri and rode northeasterly, skirting the northern suburbs of St. Louis. We did not want to have to deal with any urban traffic. Besides, that gave us the opportunity to ride back south again, following along the alluvium current of the river's flow until we reached the approach to the Illinois bridge on U.S. Highway 67.

Route 67 is of course just one number away from the famous old, and now mostly disappeared, Route 66. Similar to the more famous byway, Route 67 is a fairly major thoroughfare with lots of traffic. Instead of the mystery and romance surrounding the more famous route though, 67 is lined with a whole shipload of litter along its shoulder. And of course that's where bikes have to ride. There where countless opportunities for flat tires. Not being one to pass up too many opportunities, I rather quickly availed myself of one. The thing about this particular flat tire though, was that it was weird.

Bill, Kriss, and I were all traveling toward the bridge together. As we got nearer, the road was also bordered on both sides by trees. I pedaled along in anticipation of the opening that would provide my first sighting of the bridge. We were all paying pretty close attention to both the traffic and the trash. Evidently though, I didn't pay close enough attention to the trash.

First, I felt a slight bump coming from my front wheel. That was followed by a bigger bump from the rear. The second bump was immediately followed by a gush sound directly behind me. It was made, unmistakably, by air escaping through a narrow opening. I instinctively unsnapped my toe clips, came to a stop, and got off my bike to inspect the damage. Bill and Kriss stopped with me.

By this point in our trip, flat tires came as no big surprise and with very little disappointment. They were just a part of *doing business*. Always though, they came with the question, "What caused this one?"

I carefully inspected the tire and found no lingering debris still attached to it and there were no major holes. I took the wheel off the bicycle and the tire off the wheel. Still no evidence of what could have caused the flat. I attached my pump to the tube began to fill it with air only to discover that the air was quickly escaping through a rather huge hole in it.

"Hmmm," I thought. "No sign of any damage to the tire, but a gaping hole in the tube?" Then I took a look at the rim. There, just off-center, in the broadest part of its base, was a hole, a little over a quarter of an inch in diameter. It was as clean and neat as if it had been bored through by a high-speed drill press in a workshop.

If you are a bicyclist yourself, and have changed any number of flats, you know that this was quite an anomaly. And if you're not a cyclist, I would just want you to know that such an occurrence is just about impossible. The metal rim of my bicycle had actually been pierced through by a very sharp piece of what must have been... *God-only-knows-what.*

As cars and trucks whizzed by, the three of us nearly 60-year-old men in tight shorts and bright shirts, stood by the side of the road facing two dilemmas. First, was the question, now asked with even greater earnestness, *"What in creation caused this one?"* Second, was the question, *"How in the world do you mend a rim with a gaping hole in it?"* The first question turned out to be somewhat metaphysical with practical implications. The second was purely practical.

The practical question was the one that needed our immediate attention first and it was the most easily answered. After talking it over, we decided to go with trying to patch the rim. We cut a large swatch of rubber from the old tube. We placed it as a liner, along the center of the inside of the rim. Using wide margins, we overlapped the space where the rim used to be and was no longer. Then we put the first bead of the tire over the edge of the rim and carefully stuffed the new tube into the tire. Holding the patch in place as best we could with our fingers, we slipped the second bead over the edge of the rim and got it all put back together. We held our breath until we got enough air pressure in it is to hold everything in place. It took some finesse, but it worked. We were pretty sure that it would hold together at least until we could get to a bike shop across the river in Alton.

The other question wasn't so easily answered though. What had caused it!? During the time we had been working on the rim and afterwards, the three of us took turns walking up and down the roadside searching for any kind of object that could have caused such peculiar damage. I was even pretty sure that I knew the exact spot where it happened. Altogether, we probably spent a little over a half hour looking for whatever it was. In the end though, whatever it was remained a mystery.

With the question left unanswered, we rode on. Within just a couple of minutes we made it to the bridge. It was a grand cable span, not overly ostentatious but stylish enough. It had been newly painted and had a disposition befitting its location and purpose. As we rode across, the sun shone bright and warm through the crystalline, azure sky above. Below us flowed the muddy waters of the mighty Mississippi. Within a couple of minutes more, we had entered the Land of Lincoln. Just across, we stopped on the edge of Alton at an intersection of four busy highways, wondering which way we should go to get to the nearest bike shop.

I know it's often said that men won't ask for directions. Just the same, we did. Soon we found our way over to Fernwood Avenue on the other side of town, which was not so very far, and we walked onto Eddie's Bike Shop. Eddie's was run by Eddie himself. His staff included his best friend and a very pleasant older guy who appeared to be a relative of Eddie's. Eddie and his friend were BMX bike riders. That meant that they were incredibly talented on two wheels in ways that most people, like me, can't even understand. These are the guys you see on TV doing all kinds of gravity defying stunts. "Another mystery?" you ask. I don't know, maybe.

As an example of their agility though, when Eddie finished working on my bike, which he duly recognized as quite a unique and awesome vehicle, he asked if he could ride it. "Sure," I said. Mind you, we were in their very clutter-filled shop and store, where you even had to walk carefully so that you didn't knock anything over. Eddy jumped on my bike, rode twice through the store on a miniscule path that seemed to open and close before and after him, much like Moses and the Red Sea. Then he headed for the door which his buddy was holding open before him. A few minutes later he was back. Quite amazing!

Anyway, I explained to him the mystery of the rim-punctured flat and how I fixed it. I asked him to take a look to see if there could be a more permanent repair made. Eddie took a look inside my tire at my rim and asked, "How in the world did you do that? Nice patch job, though! I've got some good tough rim tape though, that we use to cover over old spoke holes when we swap them out for a different arrangement that might give you a stronger and lasting fix."

Like with any metaphysical or spiritual dilemma, when the possibility of asking a sage mentor arises, who would want to waste the opportunity? So, I asked Eddie if he had any idea what might have caused such a puncture. "No," he said. "That really is weird. I don't have any idea."

Afterwards, he put the tire back together, put it back on the bike, made a few other adjustments here and there, and then said, "No charge. Wow, all the way across the United States! I hope I get to do that someday."

We were off again. But the question of what had caused the flat tire in the first place remained. The enigma of my experience may not be one of the major ones, but in life it seems we are often confronted with mysteries that cannot easily solved or are altogether unanswerable. I guess, truth be told, the ones that are impossible to answer are my favorite. The idea of knowing *everything* is just way too enormous a responsibility.

Albert Einstein thought that, "The most beautiful thing we can experience is the mysterious. It is the source of all true art and all science. He to whom this emotion is a stranger, who can no longer pause to wonder and stand rapt in awe, is as good as dead: his eyes are closed." When confronted by mystery, our human response is most always an attempt to resolve it. Religions, from time immemorial, have made a fortune coming up with resolutions – in the form of theologies, dogmas and doctrines – to the greater mysteries of life.

One of my favorite authors, Tom Robbins, sums up the process this way in his book, *Skinny Legs and All*: "Early religions were like muddy ponds with lots of foliage. Concealed there, the fish of the soul could splash and feed. Eventually, however, religions became aquariums. Then, hatcheries. From farm fingerling to frozen fish stick is a short swim."

Early 20th Century, liberal, Catholic theologian, J.J. Van der Leeuw wrote, "The real mystery of life is not a problem to be solved, it is a reality to be experienced."

How often are we faced with mysteries that must go unanswered? I suspect every moment of every day. I've never met anyone who can tell for certain where or if they existed before birth or where or if they might be after dying. Sometimes I am confronted by individuals who try to assure me that they have been given divinely revealed information from inside personal sources. I'm sorry but I don't think so.

It's enough for me to have today. It was certainly enough to have that wonderful day back on May 11th. I can't do much about where I came from or where I'll end up. I can do whatever my heart, conscience or intelligence lead me to do while I'm here. When day to day questions come along that I cannot answer, I guess that's pretty good practice for the larger questions. Works for me anyway!

Poet e.e. cummings wrote, "I thank you God for this most amazing day, for the leaping greenly spirits of trees, and for the blue dream of sky and for everything which is natural, which is infinite, which is yes."

I, too, say – yes! I cast my lot with those who seek to stumble about in the dark, hoping to make the best of it... for themselves and for those around them. I cast my lot with those who seek comfort in not knowing. Since not knowing is where we seem to spend an awfully lot of time, we might just as well be as comfortable as we can be while we're here in it.

Moving On...

"To look backward for a while is to refresh the eye, to restore it, and to render it the more fit for its prime function of looking forward."   --Margaret Fairless Barber

We crossed over the Mississippi River into Alton, Illinois on the 29th day of the ride. After the brief stop at Eddie's Bike Shop, we headed back out onto the highway. As we neared University Avenue, I began to steel myself against what I anticipated would be a pretty steep climb out of the river valley. I grew up some 300 miles upstream and I was familiar enough with the precipitous ascent that had to be accomplished to get from river level up to prairie level.

I warned Bill and Kriss so that they could also muster whatever psychological adjustments they'd want to make. "Bring it on," Kriss smiled in anticipation of the challenge. Bill didn't seem to have much investment one way or the other; he was more interested in taking pictures *as he rode* of the big old homes we passed in this not so bustling river town. Much to my surprise and relief, but much to Kriss's disappointment, University Avenue required little more than a slight increase in effort. In no time at all, we were up on a bluff overlooking the Muddy Miss.

The Father of Waters was heading south out of Alton towards Memphis, Natchez and finally to the Louisiana delta. Aligning our direction with its flow, we were soon riding back down the bluff on Illinois State Route 143. There, on a very flat tract of land in the very nadir of the valley, we peeled off close to 20 miles in very little time. If I didn't know me better, I'd say it was almost effortless.

My heart was filled with a sense of comfortable familiarity, though I had never been in that particular area of the river before. My legs were filled with a sense of indefatigable stamina, even though the hour was growing late and we had already been riding for a good long while. Oddly enough, I found myself leading the pack. It was a rare experience to have Bill and Kriss struggling to keep up with me. There was no particular tailwind to help me out that afternoon, but there was no headwind either. Still, for about 20 miles, I flew like the wind, as they say.

From the age of two to the age of 20, I grew up upriver in Rock Island, Illinois. I have lots of memories of the river. I remember times as a young boy, taking the pedestrian ferry with my father from Rock Island across the river to Davenport, Iowa. Then we would turn around and take the same trip right back home again. The whole round trip could be enjoyed for price of one nickel! And I enjoyed it! What amazed me most on those ferry rides was the river's enormity. The crossing seemed to take forever, and that was good enough for me. I could've stayed out on the water all day.

I can also remember Sunday evenings when we'd go for family rides in the car. We kids would pile in, my mother would take her seat at shotgun, and my father would drive all around town. We listened to "Boston Blackie," and "The Shadow," on the car radio. Inevitably we would end up down on the river at the levee. When the water was high enough, my father would drive the car down the sloped pavement of the levee until all four tires were hubcap-deep in the muddy, swirling water. We would squeal with delight and our parents would look at each other knowingly and laugh. It didn't matter how many times we had done it before – it was great!

I remember reading Mark Twain's, "Tom Sawyer," and "The Adventures of Huckleberry Finn." We even visited Hannibal,

Missouri on a couple of one-day, sightseeing excursions. I was pretty sure that one day, I too would be a river pirate. I would go rafting about the river, sneaking aboard big paddlewheel riverboats, and experiencing untold adventures.

I was the only member of my rather large family who enjoyed fishing. I can remember summer afternoons spent lazily with friends, casting our lines out over the sea wall at the Armory. It was just a few hundred yards up from the levee where the rubber had met the water on so many earlier occasions. It was also just a few hundred yards down from the lock and damn where it was rumored that six foot long catfish lurked at the bottom. One time, I put so much snap into my wrist as I tried casting my line out as far as I could, that I lost grip of the handle. My fishing rod and reel went tumbling through the air and – kerplunk – right into the river!

I remember in my first year of high school, when all the area schools closed for a week. Teenagers and adults joined together forming ranks to mount an all out defense against the ravages of a 100-year flood. We all took our turn filling sandbags, and then standing in line, passing what seemed to be an endless supply of them, bag by bag, one person to the next, down the line to where the dike was being built or bolstered.

One night that week, I was working alongside a classmate who happened to be an All-State tight end on our football team. He was a pretty strong guy. After catching scores of successful passes from him, he caught me off guard with one. He had caught the sandbag that had just been tossed to him by the person on his other side. He pivoted, and tossed it to me, just like we'd done countless times before. This one had a little extra oomph on it though. And while *I did catch the bag*, the force of it made me fall – kerplunk –

right into the river! I was quickly fished out of the water and sent directly to the Salvation Army Coffee Truck to get a blanket and something warm to drink.

I remember going out on dates, to the movies or to a dance. In due course, sometimes those evenings too, would lead to a visit at the riverside. It was different then; the old sloping levee had been torn out after the flood. It was replaced by an impressive new seawall that ran the full distance of the downtown area. Maybe my date and I would sit on the wall and talk. Maybe we would sit in the car and talk, or do... well, what teenagers sometimes do in cars. It wasn't all that much though. Remember, it was still a fairly public place.

I remember treasured times spent by myself down on the river. Maybe I would go for a bike ride or on a long hike along it. Or maybe I would just go down to the seawall with a pad of paper and a pen. I fancied myself something of a poet and I would sit and write verses about such things as the power and the beauty of nature. Sometimes I wrote about the utility of the human construction that lined both sides of the river. Sometimes I'd write about the worlds, upstream or down, worlds that were yet unknown to me.

So on the 29th day of the ride, we crossed over *my* river into *my* home state. As we headed south out of Alton along the river bottom, I was flooded with memories of other times on that same river, up just a ways further in Illinois. I experienced that afternoon, something of an arrival, something of a homecoming.

There were still a thousand miles before we would reach our journey's end at the Atlantic Ocean in Delaware. But, even if it was for a fleeting moment, I was somewhere that I knew something about. I knew it in my bones and in my flesh and in my blood. It felt pretty damn good!

Inspirited by the company of countless memories of places not so far away, I was at home. My heart was indeed filled with a sense of comfortable familiarity. My legs were infused with the energy of an earlier and younger lifetime. And I charged ahead, full steam, with indefatigable stamina.

The adult character Kevin Arnold, whose face you never saw but whose voice you might have heard regularly as narrator on the television show, *The Wonder Years*, once mused, "Memory is a way of holding onto the things you love, the things you are, the things you never want to lose." I would only add that memory is a way of holding on to those cherished pieces, as we learn where it is we are going and what it is we have yet to do.

Moving on...

"Reach out and touch
Somebody's hand.
Make this world a better place
If you can."
--Sung by Diana Ross; lyrics by Nickolas Ashford &
Valerie Simpson

There are two kinds of people in this world. There are people who will say, "good morning," or "good afternoon," or "hello," or *whatever* to nearly anyone they meet on the street or nearly anywhere else. And then there are people who won't. I happen to be, as you might have guessed – and has been mentioned elsewhere in this book, something of an extreme extrovert. I have to greet people. It's not just my job; it's a part of who and what I am.

A slight digression here is the acknowledgement that I'm aware that some of the permission I feel in greeting total strangers is a function of privilege that comes with my gender and race. Not everyone is as safe as I am in such behavior. I wish it weren't so, but it is. So I'm not suggesting that anyone should do as I do, but I'm hoping from what I do, you can get a better sense of whatever it is you might want to do.

That said, I've been greeting people for as long as I can remember. I grew up in a smallish Midwestern town along the banks of the Mississippi River. You could walk nearly anywhere you needed to go, and I most often did. It's not like everybody knew everyone else there, but, as a boy, I was taught to be respectful of people, whether I knew them or not. To me, that meant saying, "Hello."

So, walking down the street in Rock Island, Illinois was a

great opportunity to connect with all kinds of people. I noticed early on that most often people enjoyed being addressed. They would often pick up their pace a step or sort of perk up just a little bit. That would give me a boost in return, and that was all the reinforcement I needed. Years ago, a friend of mine wrote a song that had the lyrics, "She was a goodbye woman, and I'm just a hello boy." Well, that's what I've always been, a hello boy.

This disposition has stayed with me all along, and has been a part of who I am in all the various places I've lived. In high school it was the *hello-in-the-hall* that was repeated dozens of times within the five-minute dash between classes. During my early college years, my mode of transportation was often a motorcycle. The style of greeting from one biker to another was the raised-fist, power salute. Greeting people on the El platform in Chicago on my way to work in my early 20s might have been as simple as a smile and a nod, but as often as not it also included an audible, "Good morning." (Although, I learned quickly that one had to be very careful of the little old ladies on those El platforms. They would be all sweet and pleasant-as-you-please until the train started rolling in; then you'd better watch out. If they thought the car door was going to stop and open in front of you, they'd knock you right out of their way without batting an eye.)

Years later, when I lived in rural Illinois and drove a pickup truck, I learned the traditional greeting between pickup drivers passing on country roads. There, two fingers were raised a couple of inches up off of the steering wheel. This very minimalist but visible wave was accompanied by a slight smile and almost indiscernible nod of the head. Most often this greeting was reserved for people who had known each other very well for a long time, but I was never one to stand on formalities. For the several years I lived there, I just went ahead and had a great time raising my two fingers and nodding to nearly everyone I passed. Once in a conversation, a landlord of mine mentioned to me that a good many of his friends had been asking him about that renter of his who went around waving hello to just about anybody!

Still more years and several geographical moves later, I found myself living in the metropolitan New York area. I realized that even I could not say hello to everyone. But that didn't stop me from making a serious effort. Yes, I'm a bit more careful, in my greetings now, more conscious about where I am. And I do find it daunting at times being surrounded by thousands of people. Surely there is a time and place for everything. Whenever I make eye contact with anyone though, that nearly always seems a good time and place for a greeting of some sort.

Riding a touring bicycle, especially on the road at a good clip, is not necessarily the best position from which to wave a greeting to passersby. You have to break your pedaling stride, sit up straight, take one hand off of the handlebars and raise your arm up and out of riding position. It's cumbersome; not impossible but cumbersome. That doesn't mean you don't do it. It just means you might do it more sparingly.

Sometimes on our cross-country trek, depending on the traffic, I would wave or nod or smile to trucks, cars, and people we passed. Sometimes I would just concentrate on the road and my riding. If it was at all possible though, there were two groups of people I would always make an attempt to wave to. First, if people honked and waved in encouragement as they passed, I would always try to wave back. I'm guessing those people didn't know how welcome their greetings were, but I would try to show them with my enthusiastic response.

The second group that I would go out of my way for was drivers of oncoming big trucks. Even though I was about to have my balance greatly compromised by a huge gust of wind that would come billowing in the wake of their tailgates, I would raise one arm as high as I could and wave a big, "How do you do!" As often as not, I would get a wave back or a blast from their horn in return. "Yes!" I would confirm to myself at those times.

Sometimes Bill and Kriss and I would spread out from each other over several miles on our rides. Bill is someone who has to ride fast most of the time. This is for reasons that are probably as peculiar to him as is my own need to say hello to people I don't even know. But typically that meant, if I was riding with a companion at all, it would be Kriss. If I haven't mentioned it anywhere else, I should probably note that Kriss is every bit as much of an introvert as I am an extrovert. Anyway after weeks on the road, watching me wave to all of those oncoming truckers, Kriss finally said, "They don't really care if you're here or not, Charlie."

"I know," I said. "That's one reason I think it's important to wave to them. I want them to care. I want them to know that I'm a person, and that I'm capable of reaching out to them. I want them to know, at a time when I'm not in their way and or being some kind of a hassle to them, that I am someone – just like they are."

I'm not saying that all truck drivers or even most of them are negatively disposed to bicyclists. To the contrary, most of the truckers we encountered along the way were great. But most is a long way from all. Even a very small minority of them could make a very big difference to a bicyclist. Just one indifferent or negatively inclined trucker could end a bicycle trip in a most unfortunate way. I wanted to communicate a very special greeting to truckers who might be either neutral or negative towards bicyclists. So that meant that I needed to wave to all of them that I could. None of my efforts would go to waste, though. I would merely be strengthening the bonds of connection with the ones that were already favorably disposed.

I didn't imagine that I'd necessarily ever see any of those truckers again. But I did imagine that sooner or later, somewhere down the road, every one of them would find them self driving up upon the backside of a cyclist. If I could help those drivers recognize that future cyclist as a human being ahead of time, well, all that waving would not have been in vain and it would've been a good investment on my part on behalf of cyclists everywhere.

In his first inaugural address, Nelson Mandela quoted Marianne Williamson, "And as we let our own light shine, we unconsciously give other people permission to do the same. As we are liberated from our fear, our presence automatically liberates others."

I have to tell you that I was indeed afraid of those trucks on the road. I needed to find a way of liberating myself from that fear. My meager attempts at reaching out to create a community of the road were my way of addressing that need. If my actions might help to liberate others by helping them to connect to their own humanity through a very fleeting encounter with me, that was fine too. But my goals were hardly altruistic. They allowed me, through the practice of a lifelong habit of greeting strangers, to feel connected, not only with the truckers I was waving to, but with the bicyclists they would meet in the future, cyclists whom I would never know.

Frederick Buechner, a contemporary theological scholar, whose work I'm fond of wrote, "The life I touch for good or ill will touch another life, and that in turn another, until who knows where the trembling stops or in what far place my touch will be felt."

I have to wonder what any of those truckers might have thought, had they only known the role they were playing in the unfolding of my theological evolution. I have this image in my head of one of them driving by, raising up a couple of fingers from the steering wheel, nodding slightly and saying, "Hey, that's alright, just doin' my part."

Moving on...

> "For everything there is a season,
> And a time for every matter under heaven:
> A time to be born, and a time to die..."   -- Ecclesiastes

"You know these roadways that we're riding on and all the highways everywhere are just a bunch of Dead Zones." I think my riding companion Kriss often enjoyed sounding like Eeyore. I suspect that secretly though, he harbors the heart and vulnerability of Winnie the Pooh. I'm not sure if Bill and I first heard Kriss's reference to Stephen King's, *The Dead Zone,* when he first mentioned it. It was early on in the trip but it would be repeated many more times over the course of our 46-day journey.

The truth of it is that roadways are many things. They are the arteries of commerce, networks of togetherness for families and friends. They are the rural routes of written correspondence, the superhighways of cultural connection. They are avenues of adventure for the vagabond and the boulevards of America's front and backyards. Roadways serve as many things for so many people.

But the truth of it is they *are* also Dead Zones. What roadways are to most wildlife is unsafe, and far too often fatally so. Riding a bicycle through the Dead Zone leaves one with little opportunity to deny its existence. Over the span of our trip we saw lots of roadkill. Some of it was quite fresh; some of it was rather... *not so fresh*. As often as not, when we would ride by a fallen critter, Kriss would merely call out, "Dead Zone."

While there were some consistencies among the various species of the dead that we encountered between the two coasts, there were also regional variances that were representative of the local wildlife. Early in the trip, in the mountains of southern California, there were lots of dead deer along the roadside. Through Arizona and New Mexico, the predominant victims were armadillos, an animal quite unfamiliar to this Easterner with roots in the Midwest. In Kansas and Missouri, the roadside mortality rate for raccoons, especially large raccoons, was predominant. Through the heartland states of Illinois, Indiana and Ohio, there were more dead rabbits than anything else, but there were also a good many smaller raccoons and surprisingly there were even a number of wild turkeys. Back into the mountain states, this time West Virginia and Virginia, again there was a predominance of dead deer on or near the side of the road. One afternoon in West Virginia, we saw three dead deer within just a couple of hours.

Though the Dead Zone claimed particular regional gleanings, there were two other groups of victims for which there was more than ample evidence of mortality all the way from California to Delaware. Everywhere, small birds that had been hit in mid-flight by cars, buses or trucks, could be seen lying lifeless along the side of the road. Their momentary trips and their entire lives snuffed out in an instant.

If you're traveling along at 60 or 80 mph, you might not notice. But if you are biking down the road at 16 or 18 mph, you can almost always hear an ongoing chorus of small birds singing their heart's joys and yearnings to whomever or whatever might hear them. It's quite a jarring experience, one that gives fitting pause for and entry to reflective reverence, to take in with one sense the beautiful gift of song from a particular species, while, through another sense, you are witnessing the witless demise of kin of that same animal.

The final group of victims of the Dead Zone whose lives were claimed by the road in great numbers across our entire route cannot literally be described as wildlife. That might be though, an appropriate figurative description in a number of cases. There were no decaying bodies left behind by members of this last group. Most often a simple white cross, sometimes accompanied by a bouquet of artificial flowers with fading colors, marked the spot where their lives had crossed over the line from present to past tense, from being to having been.

The difference between the human and non-human victims of the Dead Zone is that we human beings choose to engage in it. Whether by choice or by chance though, no living being is immune from its potential fatal outcome. There may be possible actions or responses that might mitigate one's odds, but nobody or nothing gets a totally free pass into or out of the Dead Zone. If you're there, you're taking a chance.

Humans do more of course than choosing to engage in the Dead Zone. We created it. It's not so odd to think in terms of creation when considering the many benefits provided by roadways. It does seem somehow sadly ironic though, to link the idea of creation with the idea of death, especially tied so closely together. And though this may seem ironic, we can't help but to know that death is an essential aspect in the ongoing unfolding stream of creation. Things/beings can't come into life, if things/beings aren't dying at the same time. It's just the way nature works.

I can't help but think that, as humans of this age we live in, we all contribute to the cause of death through the active or passive participation in the construction of an enormous highway system that mandates death. I suspect that today even a hermit would somehow benefit from this super highway system. And I don't think there are all that many hermits around anyway. That makes us all somehow responsible for the results of it, which doesn't mean it shouldn't happen, which doesn't mean there shouldn't be any roads. It does mean that there is a weight of responsibility that we all carry and which we must somehow address. We need to somehow find a way of balancing the scales.

The roadways exist and so the question we must ask is no longer, "Should we?" The question that we now face, or at least can address is, "Since we have already created Dead Zones, what do we want or need to do now to make the best of this situation?" Because the Dead Zone is a system, it may require a systematic or systemic approach to satisfy our debt. Maybe though, because we do *each* participate in it, it requires an individual response. Maybe it is both. Something, I think, is required.

We can't just go around killing ourselves and other creatures willy-nilly. There are many systems in operation in our wider culture though, that would have us believe that we can. These are systems and processes that poison our air, land and water. These structures are part of a more invisible Dead Zone and they encourage us to look only on the brighter side of convenient, modern living, and not at its costs. If we don't take some kind of responsibility for what we kill, I suspect we will just go on killing until everything is dead. Not a very hopeful prognosis, I think.

Nobel Laureate and father of the philosophy of *The Reverence for Life*, Albert Schweitzer, wrote:
   "There are only two ways to live your life. One is as though nothing is a miracle. The other is as though everything is a miracle...

"Reverence for Life affords me my fundamental principle of morality, namely, that good consists in maintaining, assisting, and enhancing life and that to destroy, harm, or to hinder life is evil. Affirmation of the world – that is affirmation of the will to live, which appears in phenomenal forms all around me – is only possible for me in that I give myself out for other life...

"Ethics cannot be based upon our obligations toward [others], but they are complete and natural only when we feel this Reverence for Life and the desire to have compassion for and to help all creatures insofar as it is in our power."

American economist, author, former Professor of the Harvard University Graduate School of Business, and political activist David Korten wrote, "If there is to be a human future, we must bring ourselves into balanced relationship with one another and the Earth."

Moving on... But not moving on too far...

Just as we can ride bicycles meanderingly through the countryside, our thoughts can wander through infinite landscapes of metaphor, leading us from the outer world to the inner world. I don't mean to set these worlds in opposition to each other, only to recognize different locations of focus. When we can see the inner and outer worlds in focus, we can see the connections that link them together.

Riding a bike on a glorious spring day can provide access to the vitality and potential for new life within one's self. Riding through majestic mountains can connect a person with their own inner sense of grandeur, and with their own connections to the larger grandeur of existence itself. Riding through a forest can put one in touch with inner strength, as well as one's often obscured untamed nature.

Just as we can meander... Where were we? Ah yes, the Dead Zone. We haven't moved on too far. Riding a bike past countless scenes of animal carnage and hundreds of memorials to human loss, as well as experiencing close calls of one's own, can certainly give a person cause to think of their own inevitable death. It sure did for me. The renowned naturalist of the last century John Muir wrote:

"Let children walk with Nature, let them see the beautiful blendings and communions of death and life, their joyous inseparable unity, as taught in woods and meadows, plains and mountains and streams of our blessed star, and they will learn that death is stingless indeed, and as beautiful as life."

I love John Muir's thought, but I have to admit that I hold the essence of his message as an aspiration, not as a fait accompli. I know, or at least I believe, that when a person dies, the significance of their death has its meaning only to the person's survivors. In the meantime though, the significance of my own unavoidable demise, while I am here and alive, is the assurity that comes with that knowledge of the vital importance of every minute of every day.

As far as I know, I don't get to do this again, this being alive. So I want to breathe in every awesome life-giving molecule of life that I possibly can. I want to breathe out – with all the gusto I am capable of – all the faith and hope, all the joy and sorrow, all the gratitude and service that I can muster. I'm going to be dead for a very long time. What I have for sure is *now*. Chicago singer and songwriter Tom Dundee wrote: "Deep within there's a feeling that time is nothing but space. Between every minute and mile that is in it, somehow there is a beautiful place."

For me that beautiful place exists in my life through the experience of love – love of my life. It includes love of my wife and family. It includes love of my congregation and all the wonderful friends – new and old, near and far – who have come into and have enriched my life. That love includes those multitudes of people that I know and the even greater legions of those whom I do not. It includes this incredible planet and all of its creatures, all of its plants and blossoms, especially the blossoms.

Does this mean I am always cognizant of those relationships, always living responsibly within them? No, I'm sorry. It doesn't. I wish I could pay attention all the time, but the truth of it is, I don't. Sometimes I need to go for a bicycle ride, or for a walk, or do something that will remind me of my mortality so that I can pay closer attention, so that I will remember that I want to pay closer attention to the love, which is the source of meaning in my life.

As she was nearing the end of her life, comedienne and actor, Gilda Radner wrote:

"I wanted a perfect ending. Now I've learned, the hard way, that some poems don't rhyme, and some stories don't have a clear beginning, middle, and end. Life is about not knowing, having to change, taking the moment and making the best of it, without knowing what's going to happen next. Delicious Ambiguity."

We all live in that ambiguity. The question is, can we embrace it? There is a time to plant, and a time to pluck up what is planted...

Once every year I lead a class for my congregation called, "Five Questions." It's an individual exploration within the context of a group process that's intended to help participants discover and articulate their own theological beliefs. In the fifth session we address the question of eschatology – what is the meaning of death? Part of the assignment for that evening is to write an epitaph. It's intended to provide an experience that might be invitingly amusing as well as self-revealing. I wrote my own epitaph for myself several years ago. I always share it with the class:

> He came.
> He saw.
> He sighed.
> He cried.
> He cared.
> He laughed.
> He left.

I know it's true; I spend much of my life thinking in aspirational terms. I don't think, at least I hope that that's not hypocritical. I think aspirations are what keep us from getting forever lost in the Dead Zone. So how about you? What is it that you hope for?

Moving on...

We stopped for lunch in Chillicothe, Ohio on day 36 of our cross-country trip. If you've never been there, Chillicothe is a pleasant little river town on the banks of the very serpentine Scioto River. It is charmingly nestled in the foothills of the western slope of the Appalachian Mountains. One of the things that make Chillicothe somewhat unique is that if you are there, and you want to get somewhere else in town, you might not be able to. The thing is that a river runs through it. Right through it! In much of the town it's nearly impossible to get from someplace on one side of the river to anywhere on the other side.

I'm guessing that for Chillicotheans it's probably much easier getting around town than it was for us. But that might not be the case. At least, that's what we were told by Jimmy, who ran the Rent and Roll Bike Shop there. "No," he answered when we asked him if we had somehow failed to see an easier route for getting to his shop. We assured him that we were sometimes quite adept at losing our way, even along very obvious routes. "It really is just about impossible to get here from the other side," he smiled. "...unless of course you're walking or biking."

We had searched out the Rent and Roll to get some minor repairs done on our bikes and to purchase a new supply of inner tubes; our best guess was that we'd gone through about 30 of them by that point. We learned from Jimmy that we were about to start some serious mountain biking the next day. "You ain't seen anything like you're gonna see tomorrow," he assured us. He informed us that all three of us needed to replace our chains. Two thousand miles had taken its toll on them and he showed us how they were starting to wear too thin. "You don't want those chains slipping around on your gears when you climbing up some of those steep slopes your about to enjoy," he said a little too gleefully but in good fun.

So we left our bikes in his grease-caked, calloused and skill-ful hands. We walked back across the foot/bike bridge over the Scioto to a remote corner of the high school parking lot, home to the Chillicothe Cavaliers. Jay Bowman, who was well into his 10-day stint as our SAG driver (and who I'll fill you in on in another chapter), joined the three of us for lunch aboard Tiggie the Wonder Camper. Afterwards, the four of us each went our own separate ways for a little down time.

I found myself stretching out in the warm, sunlit afternoon on a park bench on the bike path that followed the winding shore line of the Scioto. It wasn't far from the Rent and Roll. It occurred to me that Jimmy's was the 8th cycle shop that we had stopped into on our journey. I started thinking that our experience with him confirmed the feeling that had been growing with each successive stop at other shops across the country. Bicycle shop people are a very special, somewhat peculiar and wonderfully generous group of peo-ple!

I want to dispel a few stereotypes that might emerge in your thoughts. Bike shop people are hardly monolithic in charac-ter. They include both owners and employees. They are not relegated to a particular gender, gender orientation or eth-nicity. The ones I met along the way ranged in age from teenagers all the way up to a number of septuagenarians.

I would also encourage a few stereotypes that I found to be true without exception. The only thing that bike shop peo-ple might love more than bicycling itself – *about which they are extremely passionate* – is teaching what they know to others and doing whatever they can to facilitate their customers' rides and journeys. They are enormously generous with their time, energy and resources. I can't think of a group of people who might have been more willing to engage enthusiastically with a group of three strangers, passing through their town on a coast-to-coast trek. With each meeting of bike shop people, it was as though our adventure had become their adventure. They somehow vicariously felt that our success would also be theirs, and they were eager as could be to contribute to it.

That kind of experience began well before leaving home back in New Jersey. A member of my congregation, Michael McTigue, owner of Third Nature Bicycle Shop in Teaneck, had equipped me and given me a thorough orientation to the world of long distance biking. Bill Slezak had had the same experience with an international bicycle racer from Costa Rica, Heimer Fellas, who runs a shop named Bike Land in West Caldwell. And Kriss Wells also had a similar experience with his bike shop back in Davenport, Iowa. It was amazing how the kind of mentoring and facilitating care from bike shop people we knew back home continued without exception, with folks we didn't know at all, throughout our trip...

Early on in our expedition, we stopped one morning for a traffic light in Ramona, California. As the light turned green, we began to pull away from the curb, and the toe clip on one of my shoes broke loose from the pedal. On inspection we discovered that I was down to only one of four screws that should have held that clip in place and I only had two screws left holding on the other. Sometimes things do go well though! We discovered that we were less than a block from Kirk's Bike Shop. (Later we learned that there wouldn't be another bike shop for a couple hundred miles!) The sign on the door said Kirk's shop would open at 8:00 AM. It was already 7:45.

Kirk Newell, proprietor, lifelong international cyclist and tandem rider, arrived at about ten minutes later. He unlocked the door and let Kriss and me in. We waited quietly while Kirk went through some very serious opening rituals that he had to tend to before he could tend to us. Once he was ready though, nothing was going to stand in the way of his getting those shoes fixed and getting us back out on the road. And that was no easy task because he ended up having to match parts for equipment that he didn't even carry. He did it with aplomb and a little help from a nearby hardware store. Shoes intact once more, he bid us well and sent us on our way.

The steep ride through Prescott National Forest and finally up into Prescott, Arizona, was particularly grueling. Steep switchbacks all the way! This was the point on the trip when I recognized that I had some serious equipment issues that had to be addressed *right now*, if there was going to be any chance for me to continue at all. We found our way to the High Gear Bike Shop where Cindy Alwards took me under her care and instruction. Cindy and her husband, Steve, are co-owners of the shop. As far as I'm concerned, Cindy is something of a bicyclists' angel, not at all to be confused with a biker angel!
"My God!" she said. "These shoes are ruining your feet." She set my old shoes aside and helped me into a new pair that ended up making all the difference in the world. I felt like crying, I felt so relieved. But I didn't, at least not so as anyone would notice... I think.

I also wanted to pick up a couple of spare tires while we were there. Cindy showed me a line of teflar touring tires that had sidewalls, which came in standard black, and some spiffy ones that had red or blue stripes on them. "The question is," she asked, "do you want run of the mill? Or do you want to add a little color to your life?" I loved my new tires with their bright red stripes!

Bill had somehow severed a gear cable on his way up the mountain into Prescott. So he needed some work done on his bike, too. Kriss did too. While the guys in the shop took care of our bikes, Cindy fed the three of us grilled cheese sandwiches that she made on her brand new, electric Sandwich Master. Bodies and bikes fed and mended, she sent us happily on our way.

Two days later we made our way into Flagstaff. We didn't need any major work on our bikes this time, but we did need some adjustments. And I really needed a new saddle; my Italian leather racing seat was killing me! We stopped into Absolute Bikes, the biggest bike shop I'd ever seen. At first it was a bit intimidating. They had a huge showroom and in the shop about a dozen mechanics working on lots of different kinds of bikes all at once. When the guy working at the counter waited on us and heard about our trip though, three of the mechanics were immediately called off the jobs they'd been working on and were assigned to our bikes. About a half an hour later we were cruising on out of Flagstaff.

We received the same kind of personal care and enthusiastic service from Doug Pickett at Taos Cyclery in New Mexico. I've mentioned elsewhere the excellent treatment I received from Alan Keimig at the Tom Sawyer Bike Shop in Wichita. He was the guy who put my bike back together after my misadventure with the railroad tracks back in Kansas.

In Jefferson City, Missouri we were greeted by the man and his grandson who ran the J&D Bicycle Shop. While we had our bikes tuned-up, we were directed by the more grandfatherly fellow to something of a satisfactory lunch at the Ecco

Restaurant & Lounge, just up the street. What was particularly appealing about the Ecco, we learned from our waitress, was that it was located in a building widely known as the site of the longest running place of business in Jeff City. In fact, she assured us, it was originally constructed to provide the venue for the oldest profession, which evidently was a part of Jeff City's history during its frontier days. It was a large, substantial brick structure, so there must have been considerable thought given to securing the permanence of the brothel that had been located there!

In Alton, Illinois we found Eddie's Bike Shop. It was run by a couple of very young and knowledgeable BMX riders. BMX'ers are the hot dogs you often see on shows like Wide World of Sports. They go really fast, jump huge chasms, make looped de loops in mid air, and look like they're having a hell of a lot of fun while they're doing it. Eddie fixed the strange flat tire, mentioned elsewhere in the book, that I got as we approached the Mississippi River Bridge leaving Missouri. Afterwards, he put it all back together and said, "No charge. Wow! All the way across the United States! I hope I get a chance to do that someday." We were off again.
Beyond Chillicothe there were bike shops where we stopped in Morgantown, West Virginia and Cumberland, Maryland. Everywhere it was the same. The bike shop people didn't just want to be part of our trip; they were part of our trip. They made sure that they were.

There is an old Hasidic saying, "Everyone should carefully observe which way his heart draws him, and then choose that way with all his strength." I'm not sure if any of the bike shop people were Hassidim. If they were, they were going incognito and we couldn't tell. And I might personally paraphrase the saying to say, "Everyone should carefully observe which way there heart draws them, and then choose that way with all their strength." Just the same, all the bike shop people we met surely held true to the spirit of the old adage. They clearly loved their work, and applied to it all their strength, talent and knowledge. And then with generosity, they loved to share their work with others.

During these difficult economic times it is so heartening to know that there is an industry still going quite strong, still so full of vitality and heart, where people serve because they love what they are doing. There are some very good role models out there for the rest of us. Their example gives each of us pause to stop and take note of what we are doing – with our time and with our lives. We should be so fortunate as to find ourselves in such passionate service of others!

Moving on... Lessons from the Road

Moving On...

We ended the 37th day of our trip in the quaint river town of
Marietta, Ohio. Marietta sits boldly on the eastern bank of
the Ohio River, where it is the county seat of Washington
County. Many of its streets are lined with stately oak trees.
Waist-high wrought iron fences stand guard out front of
grand porches that give entry to intricately painted Victorian
houses and mansions. Marietta, Ohio speaks of elegance
steeped in history and community pride. With its gardens in
blossom and its trees in bloom, stepping into Marietta felt a
bit like stepping, not only into another place, but into an en-
tirely different time.

It was surprising for us to learn that in the midst of all its
grace and sophistication, that the county fairgrounds were
right there in the middle of it all, just a few blocks from the
center of Marietta. The smart folks of Washington County
realized that the grand facilities that were used for their annual fair and exposition were going unused for most of the
year. So they went and created an RV Campground in the
parking lot of the main grandstands, hook-ups dump sta-
tions and everything. There we were, just a couple of blocks
away from all that grandeur, living out of the side door of
Tiggie, on the edge of a large parking lot. *Trés elegante*!

Things were hopping all around us for a while, mostly because of the roller skating rink, which the rather clever
board of the fairgrounds had also created by putting one of
the major pavilions to use in the off-season, which of course
was most of the year. These folks were sitting on a real-
estate gold mine in the middle of town and they were making the most of it!

So, until about eight o'clock that night, our little neighbor-
hood was abuzz with teenagers coming and going. Ro-

mances waxed and waned, mostly under the glow of the parking lot's mercury lights. There wasn't much help from the new moon that was hidden somewhere aloft in the vernal night sky. The youth took little notice of the biking vagabonds off in a corner of the lot. Still, spring was in the air. They didn't seem to notice our cooking or our freshly hand-washed laundry that was hung out to dry.

After the skaters left, besides us, there were only a couple of other RV campers on the opposite side of the lot left to spend the night. Oh, and then there were also the 40 dogs that went along with those other RVs. They must have been there for some sort of dog show that had taken place earlier. The dogs were all corralled in little makeshift pens and in the early part of the evening, they made an awful lot of noise.

When we woke that next morning on our 38th day though, our early conversations were mostly filled with expressions of gratitude. From the time we'd turned off the lights and turned in for bed, we didn't hear another single yip out of all those dogs, all night long. Sleeping had been quite good, and that was usually an indicator of a good day to come. We ate some breakfast, packed our gear, checked our maps, set our route for the day, mounted our bikes, and hit the road.

The route we chose was a bit atypical of roads we normally traveled on. Interstate highways and bicycles don't mix very well, so we would always avoid those. Busy U.S. highways are better, but they're not very pleasant because of all the heavy truck and car traffic; we rode on these if there were no other reasonable alternatives. Smaller U.S. highways, many state routes and county roads were the type of roadways most favorable to bike riders and so we usually favored them. Even though they were usually good places to ride, sometimes the shoulders of these mid-sized roads had horrendous rumble strips making them not so very bike friendly. Often we'd find ourselves riding out on the highway in order to avoid them. Sometimes, that would present other kinds of issues. On day 38, we mapped out a route using only small township roads.

The day began wonderfully. Township roads aren't as insulated as larger arteries are. Pedaling past farm after farm, you really get to ride up close to rural life. It feels like you are part of the scenery that you're passing through. There were gentle rises and falls as we went rolling through the countryside, curving here and there. Now you're riding along the side of a field; now you're gliding through a dense thicket of woods. Bucolic is the word that comes to mind.

Kriss, Bill and I started the morning together, but before long we realized that this was not going to be one of those days we would spend as constant companions. Our energies were in very different places from each other's and we needed to go at different paces. We fanned out. My job of course, was to bring up the rear. In very little time we moved beyond visual contact with one another, but that didn't matter. We knew where we were going to meet up for lunch, and we would see each other then. That would be fine.

About half an hour after the last time I saw the back of Kriss's shirt, I spotted a dog on one of those nice, close porches. First the dog started barking. Then it started running. It was running across the yard... towards me, and fast. As I instinctively started to pedal for all I was worth, I began to think, "Dogs are penned up or chained on farms along bigger highways so that they won't get run over." That wasn't a problem on our little country road. Most people who passed down this road, for example, probably knew the name of this particular dog that was now chasing me.

I continued to pedal as fast as I could, all the while recognizing that this quick brown dog did not look slightly friendly and he was coming... well, he too was moving as fast as he could. I don't know how, but I somehow got out in front of him. I kept pushing hard. I was pedaling faster than I had anywhere previously on the trip, including the Rocky Mountains. I wanted to create as much distance between him and me as I possibly could. I didn't slow down for about a mile.

I've been attacked by dogs twice before in my life, both times by German shepherds. Each time I was assaulted, I got bit, hard, not only breaking through my skin, but giving me some big bruises, and I don't bruise easily. I like dogs generally; I like them a lot. I don't like the idea of being attacked or chased or bitten by dogs, though. There is nothing tolerable about it. I found that being the object of this dog's attention, on what had been such a lovely spring morning, was not only unpleasant; it was really scary.

And it happened four more times that morning before I met up with the guys again. Some of the attacks were more threatening than others. All of them were awful, as far as I was concerned. I most definitely was not going to spend any more time riding on township roadways.

"So, how was your morning?" my companions greeted me as I arrived at Tiggie's door.

"I hated it," I said. My voice was serious.

"Why? What happened?" they asked with concern.

"I spent my morning being chased by dogs," I said.

"Oh," they said, nodding their heads knowingly. And then they started to laugh! "Yeah," they assured me. "It's a drag isn't it?" And then they started laughing again.

"We saw some dogs, too," Kriss offered.

"Yeah," said Bill, "I guess they must not have seen us until we were past them though," And everyone laughed some more.

"It wasn't funny," I said. "I really did hate it."

I've been in this sort of situation before, where something nasty – maybe almost devastating or disastrous, but not quite – happens. And people respond by laughing. I've never understood that. Is it a nervous response? Is it because they hate whatever happened and they think laughter provides a response of comradeship? Is it an attempt to create a bridge from a world of crappy unpleasantness to a world that is more acceptable? I don't know.

I do know that my friends wouldn't have done anything that they thought might be hurtful. I knew that they cared for me as much as I cared for them, a lot. I know that they in no way intended to add to the difficulty of my experience. But I've got to say that I did not appreciate their reaction. I could forgive it, but I wasn't terribly pleased about it. I made my peanut butter and jelly sandwich quietly and stayed pretty much to myself through the rest of lunch. "No more township roads," I said as we started to get ready to head out.

"No problem," was the response. I always think that, "No problem," is a peculiar response anyway. But I was willing to accept it.

It's tricky sometimes, knowing how to respond to others. Bill Clinton used to say, "I feel your pain." But nobody can really feel the pain of another person. We most often diminish the experience of others when we try to pretend that we do.

We can empathize, or sympathize with others. We can have compassion for them. But if we assume we know the full extent of another person's experience, I'm guessing that we are simply missing the boat. I've got to think that's especially true if we think the other person's experience is less important than our own. Listening to the feelings that a person might be sharing with us takes us a long way towards compassion. Letting people know that we've heard what they've said might be just the balm that's needed. It might offer a kind of validation. It's easier to let go of something that's been shared when we know that it's been received.

Sometimes I think we try to minimalize a person's difficult or painful experience in an effort to encourage their comfort, or even worse to encourage our own comfort. Denying someone's experience isn't much of an affirmation of who they are. The world can be a tough enough place. When people come to us having had the *bejesus* scared out of them, maybe all they need to hear is, "Wow, that sucks!" I don't know. Call me a softie, but I hope there's a place for softies in this world.

Russian writer and social critic of the Bolshevik revolution, Aleksandr Solzhenitsyn, speaks to this experience almost as if he was there:

"One should never direct people towards happiness, because happiness too is an idol of the marketplace. One should direct them towards mutual affection. A beast gnawing at its prey can be happy too, but only human beings can feel affection for each other, and this is the highest achievement they can aspire to."

Seems like a good approach to me.   It makes for yet another excellent statement of aspiration.

Moving on...

Nearing the final days of our trip, we rode across a rustic old bridge in West Virginia. We'd spent much of the morning pedaling through some very lush and at times challenging hills when we came upon this crude and sturdy plank span. It reached from the top of one side of a cavernous ravine, way out through space, to a ledge on the opposite side. "You know," I said to Kriss as we jarringly bounced across it holding onto our handlebars like they were the handles of a jackhammer, "sometimes bridges, even really bumpy ones, are a godsend. They save one hell of a lot of pedaling and time and blood, sweat and tears." Looking over the side rails at the ravine below, I couldn't help but to share out loud my profound gratitude for the bridge.

A few minutes later when we were again rolling smoothly along on terra firma, Kriss asked, "Were you really talking about that bridge back there, or are you speaking in metaphors again?"

"Well," I said. "It really was a bumpy, rough bridge. Did you see how far down that ravine went!? It would've taken forever to ride all the way to the bottom and then have to pedal back out again! I was talking about *that* bridge." A minute later though, I had to add, "But I suppose it's that way with lots of other things, too."

Oftentimes it seems like, even though it may not be so obvious to us, there's a course we are following for getting where we want to go, for achieving what we hope to achieve. And then somewhere along the way, we might find ourselves facing a very different path than the one we had imagined. It might or might not be hard to appreciate this new route as it first appears to us. Maybe, even though it might become a more direct path for getting to where we want to go, it might be quite a bit rougher in the transition. But with fortune or grace (or however you might like to think of these things), it might in the end offer us a better course for getting where we want or hope to be.

I thought of a time years earlier when I'd lost a job, only to have it replaced with a far better one. I thought of a marriage I was in as a young man. It had been a marriage that had painfully ended, only to leave open the possibility of a far more fulfilling relationship and a healthier marriage down the road. "I guess it could go either way," I finally yelled up to Kriss. "I was talking about *that* bridge, but I guess it is a metaphor, too."

I suppose good metaphors always have their basis in real experience. And if we explore our metaphors carefully enough, they can help us to discover the spiritual terrain that we are passing through. When Kriss asked me if I was talking about the bridge or using it as a metaphor, something clicked; sometimes things do. Clouds will part and all of a sudden you can see things that are often obscured by the shadows that so often form the borders of our perceptions.

His question helped me to appreciate that nearly everything we had seen, done and experienced along our 3,000-mile trek had deeper meaning than what might have met the eye. It seemed that everything we had encountered had implications for other areas of our lives. So much of it merited our attention and consideration.

Robert C. Fuller, professor of religion at Bradley University and author of many books including, "Spiritual, But Not Religious," wrote:
    "Spirituality exists wherever we struggle with the issue of how our lives fit into the greater cosmic scheme of things.

This is true even when our questions never give way to specific answers or give rise to specific practices such as prayer or meditation. We encounter spiritual issues every time we wonder where the universe comes from, why we are here, or what happens when we die. We also become spiritual when we become moved by values such as beauty, love, or creativity that seem to reveal a meaning or power beyond our visible world. An idea or practice is "spiritual" when it reveals our personal desire to establish a felt-relationship with the deepest meanings or powers governing life."

I don't know about you, but I gotta say that I love being along for such a ride as this!

Moving On...

We spent our 38th night on the road just outside of Hundred, West Virginia. It's not so easy to know when you're outside of Hundred because it's not all that easy to know exactly when you're in it. But I get ahead of myself...

West Virginia was one of my two favorite states for breathtaking beauty. The other was New Mexico. As opposed to the craggy and often arid mountains in the West though, the Appalachians of West Virginia were round and lush, and as the man sang, "Almost heaven..."

It had been a long and eventful ride from Marietta, Ohio to Hundred. We'd ridden over 80 miles of somewhat but not horrendously challenging hills. Earlier in the morning I'd been chased by a number of unchained dogs, and that's tiring. By the time we got to Hundred, we just couldn't go any further.

We couldn't find either a motel or a campsite, so we pulled Tiggie off onto a side road and set up camp in what looked to be an abandoned field. A short while later, in the middle of our supper, we were greeted by a local fellow who rode up to Tiggie on his four-wheel ATV motorcycle. He sort of took us off guard. He was dressed in bib overalls with no shirt, a pair of work boots with no socks, and a hunting cap on his head. We are talking about no frills. I hate being guilty of judging a book by its cover, but I have to admit that visions of the movie, *Deliverance*, forced themselves into my head.

To say that we were greeted by this man is something of a misnomer. He pulled up on his ATV, turned it off and without dismounting hollered at us through the open window, "Ya can't stay here. Ya better just be moving on, now."

Right away we knew that he was right, and we promised to leave as soon as we finished eating. "Good enough," he said as he fired up his machine and took off across the field and then down the road. We all sort of sat up and just looked at each other. We were speechless for the next several minutes.

Folks in that neighborhood must've had quite a social network going because, not more than five minutes later, another fellow came along, this time in a pickup truck. He introduced himself as the deacon of the Methodist Church just up at the top of the rise, about a half-mile further. We were more than welcome to camp in the churchyard, for a fee. To say that the fee was exorbitant is really a fair assessment. But we paid it, and then felt reasonably confident that we could spend the night unmolested, which we did.

We had to get up at dawn the next morning so that Jay Bowman, our current SAG driver whose tour was coming to an end that very day, could get an early start for Morgantown, West Virginia . He needed to be there in time to catch a bus, so that he could catch a train, in order to meet up with friends in Philadelphia. It was a rather intricate plan with some tight scheduling but, if everything went well, it would work.

It had been great having Jay with us, and it was hard to see him go. But he was a young guy and it was time he had to go and do young guy things with other young guys. He would drive on ahead, and leave Tiggie where we would be able to find it at the bus depot in Morgantown.

We drove from the Methodist Church back down to the main road, West Virginia State Route 7. There, Kriss, Bill and I waved goodbye to Jay as he drove off. We hopped on our bikes and rode the few miles into Hundred proper. Hundred, West Virginia is hardly bigger than the intersection of the three highways that happen to cross there. According to the sign on the road as you enter town, it is home to 344 people. I'm not at all sure where that many people live. Hundred got its name back in the 19th Century from a couple named Church, who lived to be 109 and 106 years old respectively.

Because we had to get Jay off so early, we hadn't had time for breakfast. So we stopped in Hundred at Miss Blue's Restaurant. We leaned our bikes up against the side of the building, took off for helmets and gloves, grabbed our wallets from our saddlebags and headed inside. Because of Bill's job with the Army Corps of Engineers, he uses a wallet that shows his ID from the outside. When our waitress, who was not Miss Blue but who knew her well, saw the ID on our table, she became Bill's biggest fan. "Anybody who is a part of the U.S. Army anything," she said, "is a friend of mine." Kriss and I received residual benefits just for being Bill's companions. We all had a great breakfast.

Miss Blue's Restaurant is a regular breakfast place for many of the locals as well as for many of the truckers who frequently pass through Hundred. After our experience of having been moved on from our campsite the night before, we were trying to keep a fairly low profile. Still, we could tell that everyone in the place was listening to every word we said.

The proof of that came when we were talking about a song that had played on the jukebox. We were trying to remember the name of the person who had sung it. Kriss thought it was somebody from West Virginia, but he couldn't come up with the name.

A guy named Bob who was sitting nearby having breakfast with his father, who looked exactly like Bob except for being about 25 years older, leaned over and said, "I believe that was Bill Withers, a West Virginia boy." We knew this man's name was Bob because it said so on the nameplate of his sheriff's uniform. Both Bob and his dad stood at about 6'5" and probably weighed in somewhere around 250 or so. You could tell they were that tall even while they were sitting at their table.

The Bill Withers thing was what broke the ice. Not only did we start chatting with Bob and his father, who were wonderfully conversant and congenial, but with a lot of the other guys in the place as well. Some of them were truckers; there were a lot of log trucks on the road in those parts. Some of the guys were unemployed. Some of them had been to New Jersey. They all wanted to know about our bike trip, where we had been and where we were going.

After we'd finished our meal and we were heading for the door, on a whim, I thought it would be a good idea to ask Bob about the route we were taking. Who was going to know the area roads better than the sheriff? I wanted to know if he thought we had a good plan and to see how long he thought it might take us to get to Morgantown. It was a good thing I asked.

Turns out, for some crazy reason, that there are two different State Route 7's in that part of West Virginia. We were on the other Route 7. We weren't anywhere near where we thought we were, maybe 20 miles off. We shouldn't even have been in Hundred. I have to say, by this point I was quite glad we were. I liked Hundred.

Sheriff Bob explained, without the slightest bit of superiority, that we were lucky because we hadn't yet gone too far out of our way. If we had continued much further though, we surely would have gone way out of our way. And worse, we'd have gone up at least one very high mountain that we didn't need to mess with at all. He helped us re-chart our course, and then everyone sent us on our way. They all waved, shouted best wishes and the whole nine yards. You have to just love an experience that turns out like that.

About 10 miles up the road, one of us whose name will go unmentioned, needed to stop to use a restroom. We were in the unincorporated burg of Wadestown, which is even significantly smaller than Hundred. We stopped at the edge of town at a gas station to use their facilities. There was only one guy on duty to watch both the store and the pumps. He wasn't a local boy and didn't speak West Virginian English. He spoke almost no English at all, only Spanish.

I'm often a bit chagrined when stopping at a gas station or a restaurant to use their facilities, and I'm not planning to buy anything. I don't know, maybe it has to do with living in the New York metropolitan area where you are made to feel quite unwelcome under those circumstances. So I stayed out front with the bikes.

After a couple of minutes, I felt the guy inside at the counter staring out at me through the big front window. By that point I'm guessing he's not very happy that we've just stopped to unload, when it didn't look like we're going re-load on anything. I tried to act nonchalant, but he didn't stop staring. And then he started knocking on the window. He had to do it several times because I tried to pretend that I didn't realize that he was trying to get my attention. What the world did he want?! I didn't use the bathroom.

Once he had my attention, he started to motion for me to come inside. I pointed at my chest, and gave a facial expression that asked, "Who, me?"

"Yes," he nodded. I could see he was very excited. I've mentioned elsewhere that my Spanish is not very good and this young man had something he wanted me to know. He was speaking about it in Spanish – very fast. I was a bit slow on the uptake. Then he started pointing at my torso. I still didn't get it. So then he started pulling on the sleeve of my t-shirt. Turns out, it was my t-shirt that he was interested in.

I happened to be wearing my favorite shirt of the trip that day. It was my Toni's Kitchen t-shirt. It had been signed in indelible *Sharpie* ink by several hundred people from my congregation and from Toni's Kitchen.

Quite on his own, this young man had put together that we were on a cross-country bike ride. Now that we were on the same page, some of the verbal communication started to get easier. Looking through the window he had seen all the signatures on my shirt. He wanted to add his own to the others as a gesture of support. He had a rubber stamp that said, "Wadesville Service Station." He signed his name and then it took two tries to get the stamp to make a good clean print. He was beaming with pride and pleasure because now he had made his mark on this adventure, too.

"Y, el baño esta fácil de utilizar también. No problema!" he said. "And the bathroom is user friendly, too. No problem!" What the heck, I thought. I was already there and I might as well use it. A few minutes later we were on our way out of town, which in Wadesville occurs just as soon as you round the bend at the service station.

It had not occurred to me to ask people to sign my shirt along the way. What a great idea! Wished I had thought of it and much sooner. Even still, what a great gift it had been for this young, immigrant to welcome three scruffy vaga-bonds who are passing through his adopted home. How precious that he chose to add his name to our journey by putting it on a t-shirt that would eventually go with me to the East Coast. The whole thing made the world feel a little smaller, and a little more connected.

We still had a long ways to go that day in order to get to Morgantown, where we trusted Tiggie would be waiting for us. Lucky for us, we still had most of the day to get there. West Virginia Route 7, *the correct West Virginia Route 7*, still had lots of hills and dales and winding roads waiting for our enjoyment, as we made our way across the northern tier of the state. And we made the ride, accompanied by a host of others who were there with us in spirit.

Community organizer and author, Peter F. Block, wrote, "We are in community each time we find a place where we belong." The experience of community on the road is a most interesting occurrence. The connections have to hap-pen quickly, if they are going to happen at all. I feel like these experiences have given me the opportunity to be more open to connecting with others in the moment, when I am in my day to day life back home.

As we passed through these two West Virginia towns, we were gypsies on the move. And yet the people made room for us in their space. And for a moment, we belonged. Since my experience with them has allowed me to bring them along with me even now, who knows, maybe some-thing of us has remained with those folks too. The late artist and educator, Sister Corita Kent, wrote, "Love the moment, and the energy of that moment will spread beyond all boundaries."

Okay, maybe we shouldn't have tried to camp in the abandoned field. It was made very clear to us that we weren't welcome and didn't belong there. Maybe little marvels of connection don't happen everywhere. But it sure seems like they are a possibility more often than not. Sometimes they are if we're even just a little open to the opportunity. At Miss Blue's Restaurant and again in Wadesville, they happened for me even when I was trying to be invisible. Sometimes good things are just irrepressible.

And just in case you're wondering... Yes, Jay did make it to Morgantown on time, but barely. He'd been under the same mistaken orientation to the wrong Route 7 as us. Once he got directions and got going the right way, he got to the bus depot just in time. And Tiggie was there waiting for us when we reached town later in the day.

Moving on...

"The vocation of every man and woman is to serve other people."   --Leo Tolstoy

"Service is the rent we pay to be living. It is the very purpose of life and not something you do in your spare time."
                    --Marian Wright Edelman

"The best way to find yourself is to lose yourself in the service of others."   --Mohandas K. Gandhi

There were so many people who supported our ride across the country and our work to raise awareness and funds for hunger relief. It was amazing. And while there were so many who helped, none did so more than our team of SAG (supply and gear) drivers. Their incredible gifts of service and support given willingly, caringly and doggedly were essential to the success of our effort. Their service to us and to the ride truly made all the difference in the world.

They were a team but mostly they didn't have the benefit of working together as one. They functioned sequentially. One by one they took their turn at the helm of Tiggie the Wonder RV that was the SAG vehicle for the trip. At the end of their tenure, each driver would relay the keys to the next as we made our way eastward. Each in their own turn would take up the mantle, gauge the needs they were there to fill, and then do whatever was in their ability to meet those needs. For Kriss, Bill and me, it was an interesting and somewhat humbling experience, to watch the various ways that different SAG drivers interpreted their job, and how they participated in and added so much to our journey.

Our first driver was Dennis Barnum, Bill's brother-in-law. Dennis joined the entourage on the night before the ride actually began. As I did, he flew into Las Vegas where we caught up with Tiggie en route. He'd had some previous experience with the RV, having gone camping with the Slezaks a number of times before. The next day, Dennis drove most of the way from Las Vegas to Carlsbad. He was comfortable behind the wheel and had a puckish demeanor that was immediately disarming. He would be our *go-to-guy* for the first week.

A hallmark of Dennis's tenure was the way he would make himself available to us. Dennis had a system. He would drive about 10 miles up the road, ahead of the bikes. He would find a place to park along the side of the road that would be well-shaded for us when we got there. He would typically have chosen a spot with a wonderful view, and one that was always so obviously situated that it was easy for us to spot him. He would get out of the RV, set up his collapsible canvas chair, and take out a book he was reading. He would sit and read and wait.

As each rider caught up to him, Dennis would greet us with a big smile and whatever news there might be of the world or of the other riders who might be ahead of or behind us. He would offer us something to eat and drink, and he would question whether or not we needed any mechanical attention or adjustments. In those early days of the trip, we needed lots of mechanical attention and adjustments! He would wait until the last rider went through his temporary checkpoint and then leapfrog forward to begin the whole process again.

One of the highlights of our time with Dennis occurred on our second night out when the riders got separated from him and Tiggie, the night we got fogged in on the mountain-top in Julian, California. Dennis had gone through town well ahead of us and before the fog had set in. He had driven down the other side of the mountain, into the desert, having descended, what had been described to us as, the infamous and treacherous *Banner Grade*. He was waiting to hear from us by cell phone, but there was no cell signal to be that night in Julian.

When he finally decided to retrace his path to find us, Dennis drove Tiggie back up Banner Grade to the top of mountain. This time, he had to drive the RV into town through the incredibly thick fog that had blanketed Julian; it was no easy drive. At last, he got through and spotted our bicycles chained to the front of Margarita's Mexican Restaurant. We had already spent hours there, made friends with many of the townsfolk and had eaten a wonderful enchilada supper. By the time Dennis found us, we were knocking down a couple of Negra Models. What might have turned into a very unsavory experience for all of us, had we chosen to ride on to meet him at our planned rendezvous, did not. Dennis quickly let go of the tension that had been a part of his last several hours and joined in the party spirit. What a guy!

I want to mention here that during this first week of our trip, we were also quite fortunate to have Bill's son Jonathan along. Jonathan wasn't actually a SAG driver per se, but he sure added a lot of support to the trip. At 25-years-old. Jonathan is smart, good-looking, strong and lean. He has a wonderful can-do attitude, and is one of the most technically savvy people I know in this age of the electronic superhighway. I, on the other hand, am one of the *least* technically savvy people I know.

I had been very hopeful of staying in touch while away with the folks back home. That left me relying heavily on Jonathan, not only for his tech abilities, but for teaching us what we would need to do once he left us at the end of his week. The latter task being his greater challenge!

We were way out there in terms of Internet connections, GPS positioning, transferring files from cameras to computers and back again, making videos to send back home for presentations or getting blog materials up on the Internet. Whatever we needed him to do, Jonathan would figure out how to do it, and then he would make it happen. And, by the time he left, we sort of understood what we needed to do. Again, what a guy!

On day seven of the ride, we were joined in Prescott, Arizona by Martha Easter Wells, Kriss's wife. She had about 24 hours to learn what she could from both Dennis and Jonathan. They would be leaving us the next day in Sedona when we reached the other side of the Prescott National Forest and the Prescott-Jerome Waterway. Unlike Dennis, Martha didn't have the benefit of previous experience in Tiggie. In fact she didn't have experience driving anything larger than a pickup truck. But she was a fast learner with an *I can do anything* demeanor that allowed her to get way more done than not.

Martha would be our SAG driver with the longest tour of duty. She would be with us all the way from Prescott, over the mountains, across the plains and into the prairie states of the Midwest, all the way to Mulberry Grove, Illinois. She contributed three weeks of her time, effort and caring, as she drove over 1,500 miles. It was not the trip that she had planned on, but it was the one she made the most of.

Lots of times, beforehand, we have ideas about how things are going to be and then of course, they turn out altogether different. Martha had thought that being our SAG driver would mean saying, "Goodbye," to us each morning as we started our day's excursion. Then maybe she would meet up with us for lunch and finally, she would gather us back in at the end of the day's ride. Her expectation, being something of an expeditionary hiker, was that she would have plenty of time and freedom to get in some very serious walking while we were doing our serious riding.

Like I said, Martha was a fast learner and she really could do almost anything that she set her mind and heart to. In this case, she realigned what she thought was going to happen with the new information she perceived about what was needed. Then she came up with a new plan. To a very considerable extent, she sacrificed her ambition of three weeks with plenty of walking in order to support Kriss, Bill and me on our ride.

Similar to Dennis, her pattern was to leapfrog ahead of us. She would drive 10 to 15 miles ahead and park along the side of the road. So that she wouldn't have to totally forfeit her aspirations of ambitious ambulation, she would find interesting country roads or trailheads to park near. Her hikes were much shorter and broken up than she'd anticipated, but she was still able to hike what must have amounted to hundreds of miles while she was with us. She was able to get some of what she needed, and we always had access to whatever we might need.

For me, the highlight of Martha's tenure was one of my own low points. It occurred when I crashed my bike while crossing the railroad track in Kansas. Not only was my bike banged up and unridable, so was I. Martha pretty much got me through that experience, nursing me along and lifting my spirits from that nadir, so that I could get back into the ride.

It wasn't so much that she was there to help pick me up shortly after the accident occurred. It wasn't that she got me into the RV and set out for the hospital. It wasn't that she masterfully handled pulling our huge vehicle safely to the shoulder when we blew out the left rear dual tires on the way to the hospital. It wasn't even the way she calmly managed to arrange for a service truck to come out and re-pair the RV, or the way she acquired an alternative ride to get me to the hospital.

It was much more the way she cared for me, once I was re-leased from the ER and for the next couple of days while I was in pretty bad shape. We sort of became housemates in Tiggie for those couple of days, and Martha made sure that I was as comfortable as possible and that I had whatever I needed. Florence Nightingale, Clara Barton and Margaret *"Hot Lips"* Houlihan would have all been very proud. I, on the other hand, was very grateful.

In retrospect I have to wonder about the challenge it must have been for Martha to abide living with three grungy, road-focused, not always on our best nor most sensitive be-havior, men in such close quarters for three weeks. Hell, that's a lot to say, let alone live with. She did it though! Martha was able to put up with us, as planned, all the way up to our first night in Illinois. There, in Mulberry Grove – which, yes, did have a strong resemblance to Mayberry RFD! – she handed the keys off to Jay Bowman, who had driven down to join us from Davenport, Iowa.

Some history about Jay... my daughter, Shana, the Wells' daughter Linda and Jay Bowman were Sunday school class-mates at the Unitarian Church in Davenport. They were buddies there from the time they were babies until the Ortman family left for Massachusetts; that was about the time the three of them were all eight years old. Through electronics, actual visits and however else they could, they have continued to be close friends over the 20 years and the thousands of miles since then.

The summer before our bike ride, the three of them were responsible for conducting a five-day seminar on social activism in Amman, Jordan. It was held for NGOs and other entrepreneurial groups, both from the Middle East and from around the world. It was held under the auspices of the United Nations, where Jay was employed. By the time he joined us on our bike ride, Jay had left his position at the UN and was enjoying a little downtime before the onset of his graduate studies at the Hubert H. Humphrey Institute for Public Affairs at the University of Minnesota.

Although I knew of him, I hadn't really known Jay since he was a little boy. Now he was 25, bright, well-read, something of a bicyclist himself, and full of what we used to lovingly call back home, *piss and vinegar*. He was up for an adventure with some good *old* boys, and we were up to having him along. Jay was a joy to have on board! To say that he gave a great boost to our journey some 30 days into it, would be a significant understatement.

Jay's style of caring for us was much like Martha's had been, and Dennis' before her. He would often leapfrog ahead of us, but instead of pulling out of picnic chair or going for a hike, he would jump on a spare bike we brought along and do some serious riding himself. Sometimes though, he would stay inside Tiggie and read one of the many books he'd brought along on the trip.

During Jay's term of residence, the four of us got along quite well. We would engage in conversation over lunch, dinner, or nighttime card games of euchre. We might talk about international or national politics or history, theology, philosophy or religion. Sometimes we would talk about the generational differences in our coming-of-age processes. Of course, lots of times we would simply take pleasure in totally inane or mundane banter as well. We would share stories, drink beer, laugh a lot and generally enjoy each other's company. It was good for all of us. I'll cherish those memories as I get to watch what I'm sure will be a most promising future for Jay.

Because of logistics and timing, it turned out that Jay had to leave us a day before his SAG relief arrived. He wanted to catch a particular train that would get him to Philadelphia in time to meet up with a bunch of college friends. As a result there was somewhat of an awkward handoff of the keys for the last leg of the journey. Bill tried to both drive and ride the same amount of miles that day, but it didn't go all that smoothly. We ended up spending much of the morning of that 40th day of our trip in Morgantown, West Virginia. It's not that we wanted to stay in Morgantown; it's just that we kept going around the mountains in huge nonproductive circles. We got lost and frustrated. By the time we met up with our new drivers, two lovely women from New Jersey who decided to make the trip as a team, we were quite ready for their company.

There were by this point, although we had no way of knowing it, only seven days remaining before reaching the Atlantic Ocean at Bower's Beach, Delaware. My wife, Judy, would be with us for five of those days and Bill's wife, Rickey, would see us through until we reached the sand and foam, which was our goal. Having two out of three of our wives with us at the same time changed the trip in some ways, but then each of the new SAG drivers – all across the country – had brought with them their own personal styles and changes. So in many ways, things continued much as they had all along. Our days were spent riding and our nights were spent enjoying food, drink and each other's company.

Call me an irrepressible romantic, but I found Judy's company to be a delight, and Rickey's too. Besides their unique companionship, they took on their jobs in much the same way as those who'd gone before them. Their ambition was to take care of our logistical needs so that we could ride.

It's pretty amazing that all our generous drivers could see value in what we were doing and wanted to be a part of it by lending a hand. 17th Century English poet, John Milton, wrote, "They also serve who stand and wait." While none of our SAG drivers stood in any one place for very long, they did wait. They waited *for* us and they waited *on* us.

I only hope it was as good for them as it was for us. I put trust in the words of Ralph Waldo Emerson, "It is one of the most beautiful compensations of life, that no [person] can sincerely try to help another without helping [them self]." And I put faith in Helen Keller's words, "Happiness cannot come from without. It must come from within. It is not what we see and touch or that which others do for us which makes us happy; it is that which we think and feel and do, first for the other fellow and then for ourselves."

SAG drivers are special people. They are the unsung heroes of any major bicycle trip or bicycle race. They are cooks, mechanics, gophers and nurses. They are cheerleaders, companions, humorists and humanizers. They are the adhesive that holds it all together. They are the difference between a cyclist being a rider or having to engage in myriad other tasks that are not about riding. I say, thank goodness for SAG drivers, and especially thank goodness for the team that was ours.

Moving On...

Some people say that familiarity breeds contempt. I couldn't disagree more. That is of course unless that with which you are growing familiar happens to be contemptible, but even that would have to be a matter of perspective. Familiarity is what comes from being attentive and present to the experiences of our lives.

Familiarity was not a contemptuous matter on our cross-country bicycle trip. The more that I got to know my riding companions, Bill and Kriss, the more I came to appreciate them as comrades in the quest for self-discovery and discovery of the world itself. Another thing, as it turned out, was that we ended up riding a good number of miles on a biking trail that I was quite familiar with. Far from contemptuous, I was delighted to share this familiar experience with my friends.

The Great Allegheny Passage Trail, built on old railway bed, runs 160 miles from Pittsburgh, through the mountains of Pennsylvania, over the top of the Eastern Continental Divide, and finally down into Cumberland, Maryland. Many times in recent years, when I could steal away for a bit of R&R, I'd strap my bike to the back of the car, head down to Ohiopyle State Park in southwestern Pennsylvania, for a few days riding on the Great Allegheny.

I loved it. The trail provides mile after mile of Appalachian beauty. I've ridden on it for days in the spring when entire mountainsides are filled with trillium in blossom, and in the autumn when those same landscapes are ablaze with fiery foliage. The Passage follows mountain streams and forests, crosses old wooden bridges and great huge viaducts. It passes through picturesque farmland and quaint mountain towns. The most exquisite thing about it though, is that because it was built on rail bed, the pitch of any ascent rarely, rarely exceeds 3%. It was made for my kind of biking!

Back home, when we were in the planning stages of our trip, I had hoped we might be able to ride on the Allegheny. As our route began to take shape though, it looked doubtful. We would probably be much further south at that point, and it looked like we would need to go pretty far out of our way in order to use it. Out of the way was out of the question; on that we all agreed.

But then when the trip was well underway, as we came across the state of Ohio, we began to feel disenchanted with the *Race Across America* route that we'd been using. Their route used a lot of big highways. While those roads had wider shoulders and might have been particularly favorable for biking speed, they were also much more heavily trafficked, especially by big trucks. They weren't all that pleasant for long periods of bicycle riding.

We started mapping out some directions of our own. Before long we were riding north along the banks of the Ohio River. Before much longer, we were heading on a course that would intersect with the Great Allegheny Passage Trail, which we could meet at about the midpoint of the trail, somewhere between Ohiopyle State Park and Confluence, Pennsylvania.

My hopes for introducing Bill and Kriss to this wonderful experience were rekindled, but I had some misgivings. Hard surfaces are typically the best bet for long-distance bicycle riding. We hadn't really ridden on any non-paved trails, although we had tried a few miles on the Katy Trail back in Missouri. That trail proved to be much too soft. Soft doesn't work well, especially with the very skinny tires on our touring bicycles.

"I don't know if this will work or not," I said. "But whenever I've ridden on it in the past, the very tiny limestone gravel chips have been packed tight and solid. We could try it for a few miles and if we are able to ride on it, I don't think you'll be disappointed."

So on the morning of our 41st day, we set out on the Great Allegheny Passage at Confluence. We headed off into the woods, the hills and dales, over the rivers and through the tunnels. It wasn't just that the trail worked, it worked incredibly well. The surface of the trail was in excellent condition. We were able to zoom along at a clip that would match any highway riding that we had done.

The minimal grade elevation allowable for the old locomotives created a Valium-like effect on the terrain; the non-productive peaks and the valleys were gone. Even though it felt like we were mostly riding on a level surface, we were actually climbing our way up to the top of the Eastern Continental Divide. We rode up through the little towns of Rockwood and Garrett. Then, just before reaching Meyersdale, we crossed the most amazing bridge that spanned almost from here to forever. The Salisbury Viaduct is 1,952 feet long. It arches over four sets of railroad tracks, six separate roadways, some huge pastures and fields, and a couple of waterways. The view from out in the middle of the viaduct seemed more like that from an airplane than from a high floating structure somehow secured to the ground.

The segment from Meyersdale to Frostburg might be the most incredible part of the whole Alleghany Trail. It was filled with surprises for Bill and Kriss and I loved introducing them to it all. First, we crossed the Mason-Dixon Line, an actual place marked with a commemorative sign, just at the border, leaving Pennsylvania and entering Maryland. Only a few hundred yards from there, we crossed over the Eastern Continental Divide at the height of 2,392 feet above sea level. It was about 10,000 feet lower than the other Continental Divide that we'd spent days scaling in New Mexico. It was quite okay with me that we didn't have to do anything like that again.

From the Divide, we started riding downhill. If the climb up had been accomplished easily, going down the eastern slope was even easier. The next event was Big Savage Tunnel, which is well over a half mile long at 3,297 feet. Every few hundred yards, there would be a low wattage light bulb hanging on a wire from the wall, but we surely couldn't see from one light to the next. The tunnel was so dark and so long, it created an otherworldly feeling, like I was riding effortlessly and weightlessly through space. It was quite surreal.

Another mile later and we rode into Borden Tunnel, only 960 feet. In comparison it might have been much shorter, but because of that, they didn't bother with any light bulbs, at all. It was easily just as dark as the longer tunnel, and created just as dreamlike an experience. It was a very spiritual for me. It made me think that following my death, one day long from now I hope, if there is an afterlife, mine might be spent riding my bicycle joyfully through the darkness of space, visiting one planet here and then maybe a star far off over there. I don't know, but if there is an afterlife and that's what it's like, as long as I get to meet and be with others on such a journey, that's okay by me.

Soon after the tunnels, we were in Frostburg. The weather started to change and the temperature dropped a few degrees. A light rain started to fall. By the time we got to Cumberland, the gentle rain had turned into a pretty good downpour. Our SAG drivers, Rickey and Judy, were waiting for us there at the train station. As we came rolling into the depot, we were so drenched and caked with mud that someone might have a hard time telling us apart. Okay, so our wives knew who we were... Fortunately, we had access to the depot restrooms, and more fortunately, we had them all to ourselves. When we emerged, we were clean and – even if we weren't pretty – we were easily recognizable again.

There was now something less than a week left to our trip. It didn't feel like the end, but it was starting to feel like the beginning of the end. There were still many decisions that had to be made. How would we plot our course around the Washington, D.C. area? Should we go right through the heart of town or should we avoid that at all cost? Should we stop to see friends that we knew or did we need to stay focused? Annapolis really isn't at the ocean, is it? What would be the roads we would choose for the last stretch?
Alice came to a fork in the road. "Which road do I take?" she asked.
"Where do you want to go?" responded the Cheshire cat.
"I don't know," Alice answered.
"Then," said the cat, "it doesn't matter."   --Lewis Carroll, *Alice in Wonderland*

It wasn't so much that we didn't know where we wanted to go. We'd come a long ways by now and we wanted to make it all the way to the Atlantic Ocean. Although we did have some latitude as to exactly where that might occur, in the end it probably would not matter exactly what route we'd take to get there.

What would matter would be that we would want to live into whatever experience we might find ourselves a part of. We would want to share that experience with each other.

We would want to continue to grow in familiarity *and* in appreciation.

One thing that we'd been learning on our trip was that nothing lasts forever. Not the trip, not us. And so, if we were going to glean from all this manna of experience that we kept finding along our roadside, we needed to pay attention to where we were at least as much as to where we were going. We didn't know how much time we had left, but we did know that we had *now*. If someone is being honest about it, *now* really is a lot to hold on to.

13th Century poet and Sufi mystic Rumi wrote, "The Guest House," as an invitation to being present with all the experiences of our days and our years:
"This being human is a guest house.
Every morning a new arrival.

A joy, a depression, a meanness,
some momentary awareness comes
as an unexpected visitor.

Welcome and entertain them all!
Even if they're a crowd of sorrows,
who violently sweep your house
empty of its furniture,
still, treat each guest honorably.
He may be clearing you out
for some new delight.

The dark thought, the shame, the malice,
meet them at the door laughing,
and invite them in.

Be grateful for whoever comes,

because each has been sent
as a guide from beyond."

I'm not sure about guides from beyond. I don't know if we find meaning in our lives, or if we make it, or both. I suspect it's something of the latter. What I do know is that, while we're here, the opportunities for engaging in life are endless. There's little chance of ever running out of new experiences to embrace and to learn from, new textures to feel, new meanings to share, new ways of responding to life, ways that give back to it and that make our life more full.

Moving On...

So what we do with our lives
We leave only a mark.
Will our story shine like a light?
Or end in the dark?
Give it all or nothing.
  -- From *We Don't Need Another Hero*, by Tina Turner

We arrived at Parole, Maryland on May 27, our 45th day out. It was the evening before what would be our last riding day. We were welcomed to the home of Kathy and John Clay. Kathy was an old friend of Bill and Rickey's from the Unitarian Universalist Mid-Atlantic Conference (UUMAC), an annual summer church camp held in the Pocono Mountains of upstate Pennsylvania. Kathy was still at work when we got there. No big deal, John, who had never met any of us prior to our appearance that day on his doorstep, welcomed us in as though we were some kind of mythical heroes. I've recently read Seamus Heaney's version of *Beowulf*, and I knew we weren't.

As far as I could see, we looked like a gaggle of grungy and grizzly riders – quite rough around the edges and in the middle too. After a month and a half of life on the road, even our own mothers might not have recognized us. Still, John managed to convey quite clearly that he was particularly honored that we had chosen to spend this night in his home. I guess beauty, as well as other forms of appreciation, really does lie in the eye of the beholder. He took us in.

Our rehydration was quickly accomplished with a couple of cold brewskies. Then it was off to the showers where there was plenty of hot water and soft towels to follow. Bathing and shaving encouraged the return of that good old feeling of being a member of the human race again. Next, we went downstairs to find a a table filled with luscious hors d'oeuvres, pleasing libations and a seemingly endless supply of adoration from John. He was so daunted by our having undertaken such a journey and impressed that it was nearly complete. 19th Century American novelist, Nathaniel Hawthorne, once noted, "A hero cannot be a hero unless in a heroic world." John did a pretty amazing job creating heroic world, with all of us in it.

His appreciation, along with my own growing assuredness that we would soon reach our goal, allowed me to start thinking about the larger picture of what it was that we had almost completed. I wasn't really thinking about what a great accomplishment this all was. I was thinking about how grateful I was to have survived it.

Flashback... The day before leaving on the trip, I went into my office at the church, back at home. I needed to get a few things ready for the Easter services the next morning. While I was there, I sat down at my desk to write a couple of letters. I wrote them, sealed them in envelopes and left instructions for my associate minister... just in case.

I fully expected to come back from this journey that I was about to set out on. But what if I didn't? What if something did happen? What if I didn't make it back? The least I could do, it seemed, was to leave a couple of messages, again... just in case.

I do a lot of writing in my line of work, and I have written many things that I hope will still be around, at least for a while, after I'm dead and gone. But I have never written something that was actually intended to be read posthumously. It was something of an awesome and daunting task.

The first letter was to my wife Judy and to our kids. I just wanted them to know how much I loved them and how much I appreciated having had them in my life. I told them that I hoped they wouldn't be too angry that I had gone on this trip at all. I explained that it was about being alive, and that if they were reading the note because I was dead, I hoped that my having died while being fully engaged in living would be of some consolation to them. What I didn't write, but did suppose, was that they'd still be a bit pissed anyway. I hoped my note might mitigate that. I also wrote a few other things I wanted them to know.

The other note was for the congregation. I wanted them all to know how much I appreciated the time they had given me to go on this trip. I told them how having been their minister had helped to shape my life in so many meaningful ways. The letter also included some thoughts about my memorial service – nothing terribly morbid, just favorite hymns they might include and that sort of thing.

The provocative French-Cuban born author and screenwriter, Anaïs Nin, once wrote that, "People living deeply have no fear of death." Easy for her to say! She was probably not in the process of writing letters like the ones I've just described.

It's not that I was wracked with fear or anything like that, not by a long shot. A healthy respect with a dash of trepidation is how I would describe my thoughts about death as I was about to embark on this *experience of deep living*. The letters I wrote that day are still in my desk drawer in my office at the church. They are an honored memento for me of that particular moment in time.

Flash forward, but not all the way back to Day 45... I had known before the trip that my wife Judy struggled with fears of me not making it back, too. She was a trooper though. She was not going to let her fear get in the way of supporting my desire to undertake this odyssey. Now that's love!
On one of our phone calls early in the trip, she said, "I'm not afraid anymore. I know everything is going to go fine."

When I asked her how she knew this, she said, "It came to me when you guys made it safely to the top of the mountain in Julian, the day the fog set in. You were warmly treated in the restaurant, and eventually Dennis found you even though the communication and visibility were awful. You said that if you had proceeded down the mountain, as you had planned, you would have been in serious trouble. I figured the gods were on your side."

After she said that, I decided that I'd wait to tell her about almost being blown off the mountainside by the nasty, California semi truck driver on the first day of the ride. She didn't need to know about that until we were together face-to-face. It was better that way.

Flash forward again to Day 45... So I don't know if my new friend John Clay was contemplating his own mortality, or ours, or just what he might have been thinking. I knew that he revered our journey, not out of envy and not voyeuristically, but with a sense of identity. I think he imagined himself doing something like what we were doing. I hope he is still working on what it will be.

By the time Kathy got home from work, we were ready to sit down to dinner. John had prepared a beautiful table and a scrumptious meal of some kind of chicken that he'd cooked in a pressure cooker. I'd never had anything like it before. He was quite proud of it and we were very fond of it!

I had taken several ball caps with me on the trip. One of my favorite caps was from back home and it read, "NEW JERSEY: Keep Every Day Real." I gave the hat to John as a token of appreciation for his phenomenal hospitality and as a token of friendship. But I also gave it to him as recognition of the importance of his dreams, and his ability to make those dreams come true. He seemed to be moved by the gesture and I was pleased.

We were joined that night by a host of others who came to the Clay house. Bill and Rickey's son, Jeremy (whom I've known since he was a young boy and have had the privilege of watching grow into a most enjoyable and determined young man) and his girlfriend, Kacee, had driven out from their home in Washington, DC. There were some others from the UUMAC community that joined in too.

The party went on way into the night, well after my ambition or capacity to keep up with it endured. It had already been a long day. And tomorrow, well tomorrow was going to be one more day.

Moving On...

"And in the end, it's not the years in your life that count. It's the life in your years." --Abraham Lincoln

When I woke up on our 46th day, the day we would make it to Bowers Beach, I was rather amazed and glad that the party animals that had been up into the wee hours of the night were able to get up and get moving, too. John and Kathy's gracious hospitality continued through a more than ample breakfast and a hearty farewell.

John had helped us to map out our course for the day. "If you go this way," he suggested, "you'll avoid a lot of residential areas and you'll be in the woods through most of the Outer Bank. There's often a pretty stiff wind that comes blowing in off the ocean. I'd guess those trees will make a good windbreak. That'll make for a pretty pleasant home-stretch for you guys."

We waved goodbye and, with growing ambition for reaching the *end of the trail*, we set out. We would get to the Outer Bank in the afternoon. Before that, in the morning, we would be in Annapolis, the capital of Maryland.

If you've never been to this historic city, which I had not, it'll charm your socks right off. We stayed there long enough to soak up a bit of the atmosphere in the downtown and harbor areas, and to appreciate the colonial elegance of the old capital district. We were also there just long enough for poor Rickey to get Tiggie caught up in a traffic jam. There were lots of tourists in town, with lots of other RV's and they all kind of helped each other to get into the spirit of vacation – slow moving!

From the city we headed north to the William Preston Lane, Jr. Memorial Chesapeake Bay Bridge, the only access to the Outer Bank on the lower end of it. The name of the bridge is quite a mouthful, but that was nothing in comparison to the 4.3-mile span of this elevated skyway over the huge body of water that is the Chesapeake Bay. The only problem was that the bridge was part of the interstate highway system, and it was illegal to ride bicycles on it.

We threw our bikes onto the racks on Tiggie and drove across it. Once we saw the amount of traffic that was on it, we were grateful that we weren't out there trying to avoid the speeding cars and trucks. There was no way we would have wanted to ride across that bridge, and there was no way that we'd have made it. When we got to the other side we stopped, had a bite of lunch and then began our final run to Bowers Beach.

It was a beautiful afternoon with sun-filled skies. We could feel the breeze blowing across the landmass from the ocean. It was impossible to avoid it. It didn't take us long to realize that John's guess that the trees and woods would provide a windscreen – was just a bit off the mark. I'm not saying that the winds were 40 miles an hour. But I would guess that some of the gusts might have been as strong as 30. And of course the wind was coming off the ocean, while we were riding towards it.

I don't know but somehow it seemed fitting that our final afternoon would be spent riding into a substantial headwind. Sometimes the world seems more right when particular conditions prevail. Riding into the wind my mind drifted a bit... Back home at the YMCA there is a group of older guys who play volleyball on Friday mornings at 6:45. Some of the same guys have been a part of that game for over 30 years. Every Friday morning, when I come up from the locker room on the way to my workout on the cross-trainer machines, I walk past the gym where their game is in progress. And every week as I do, I have the feeling that, as long as that game is going on, there are at least some things that are right in the world.

Riding into the wind the rest of the way to Bowers Beach gave me that same feeling. Of course, it also made me work... hard. None of this easy finish stuff for me. And that was just about right.

Kriss and Bill wanted to lay it all out on the road. They had no need to hold anything back in reserve. This was it – the real deal. I wanted to do the same thing, but the result of those same desires in me didn't quite net the same outcome. I tried to keep up as best I could, but that didn't last long. "You guys go ahead," I said. "I'll see you a ways up the road." They pedaled on ahead, taking turns drafting and leading. I was able to watch them from behind for a little while.

I would have enjoyed keeping up with them too, but just the same, I found myself feeling content to have a couple of hours to myself. It gave me some time to appreciate this last day and the other 45 days that had preceded it. It had been quite an undertaking. I found myself not knowing how to think about it.

After a while, I crossed the state line and was in Delaware. Not knowing how to think about something so enormous, I began to focus on how I felt, and then a number of feelings and thoughts began to emerge...

I thought about other states I'd been in, about how hard the western mountains had been, how beautiful the deserts where. I thought about the flowing rivers and their lush valleys, and about the magnificent forests. I thought about the

Brewbaker's, Jolene and Max, Steve Burke, all the great bikeshop people, and so many others, and I couldn't help but to feel grateful for the pieces each of them had added to the journey.

I thought about our suppers in Tiggie, about our card games that sometimes went well into the night, and about some of the funny things that happened and made us laugh until we cried. I thought about being able to eat as much ice cream as I wanted. I thought about our gracious SAG drivers. I thought about how, even in some of the hardest times, I was so glad to have been a part of such a phenomenal and grand expedition.

I thought about the physical pain I had endured. If I had known beforehand just how much there was to be, I probably wouldn't have taken the ride. I thought about how glad I was that I hadn't known, about how pain is really just another experience that goes into the hopper in the growing of a soul, like grist for the mill. I thought about how grateful I was that I'd had such an opportunity as this.

I thought about the reality of heading home the next day. We wouldn't be heading to the same homes though. We would be heading, each to our own. Author Roberta Israeloff wrote:
"In the end we are all separate: our stories, no matter how similar, come to a fork and diverge. We are drawn to each other because of our similarities, but it is our differences we must learn to respect."

I don't know if in the end we are really separate or if we somehow we remain connected, in a very real sense, to every experience and every person we may have shared our experience with. I know that we do remain connected, but there is always some sort of separation that is also real when an experience ends. On our trip, we had learned something of respect – for ourselves and each other, for the precarious and precious balance of life, for our varying abilities, for holding up our ends of the deal, and for working to turn the potential of a dream into lived experience.

Bill and Kriss had recognized the importance of our crossing the finish line together. They held up and waited for me when they got within a couple of miles of it. I was glad they did. As we got to the beach, I wanted to feel our connection as keenly as possible.

It was a fairly quiet but comfortable few miles. There wasn't much said, nor that needed to be said. Our time of sharing this adventure was just about over. The smell of the ocean air was growing stronger and we watched for our first sighting of water.

Rickey had driven on ahead in Tiggie. She was waiting for us to join her at the path that led through the beachgrass, down to the shore. With camera in hand, she was ready to record the historic moment. The sun was setting behind us, over the continent we had just traversed, as we dismounted and carried our bikes across the beach to the water's edge. You wouldn't want to get a lot of sand in your chains or gears; that just would not be a fitting end. There wasn't anyone on the beach but us, as we stepped to the water and set our bikes down. The gentle slap of the early evening ebb tide broke over the rims of our wheels.

Bill grabbed a camera so that he and I could record one more video message for the folks back home, so they could see and hear this moment on the blog site. I talked for a bit about the sense of achievement that we were experiencing and about how that sense was so fleeting, even within that moment. I spoke of how we'd gotten to know ourselves and each other so much more deeply for the experiences and the miles that we had endured and shared. I talked about how it was too early to know what it all meant yet, but that I expected it would continue to unfold for us as we thought back on our trip, and that we would still have plenty to learn that would come out of our ride.

I am forever an old softy, sometimes embarrassingly so. Sure enough, I choked up while I was speaking into the camera; tears came to my eyes. In retrospect, it sort of reminds me of times I have seen a great tennis match end with the champion kneeling down on the court in tears. I was so glad to have made the trip, so incredibly grateful.

Even then, I was not at all sure that I was glad it was over. If the ocean had not been there, I think I would have gladly continued riding. But 3,015 miles would have to be enough, at least for now.

Epilogue...

"I still find each day too short for all the thoughts I want to think, all the walks I want to take, all the books I want to read and all the friends I want to see."
--John Burroughs

Off to the edge of the beach we found an unattended public restroom and managed to clean up, not minding too much that it was in a cold-water shower. Another hour later and we were sitting around a table at Frenchies Dock Restaurant, just a few blocks away. The beer and the wine had been poured and we were chowing down some excellent and very fresh seafood. After awhile, I asked the guys, "So, what were some of the best things for you?" Here are just a few of mine...

The best shower was at a campground in Taos, New Mexico. There were only two showers and you had to wait for one to open up, but when it did it was worth the wait. Each of showers was in an individual room, decorated stylishly in a Southwest desert motif. It felt like you were someplace where people cared about what they had to offer. But the best part was the shower itself. It was enormous and had a bench in it, where you could just sit. There was an endless supply of steaming hot water, and it was the perfect way to end a long day of biking in the desert.

The best meal was a community potluck supper with some friends we'd just met, the Brewbakers, who were part of the German Brethren of the Anna Baptist Church in Sawyer, Kansas. Being honorary members of their community for one night was one of the greatest privileges that I've ever experienced. That the food was excellent and endless did not detract from the experience.

The best moment, and I'm not absolutely sure there was only one best moment because there were so many exceptional ones, but one that stands out for me now, was when I met Steve Burke in Greensburg, Kansas. It was not only the impact of meeting this person whose story I had told after hearing about it on National Public Radio, at home 1,500 miles away. What was most meaningful about it for me was that it was an actual instant in which several worlds came together. It was a moment of synchronicity that was filled for me with tenderness and appreciation.

The best bike shop, *and they were all outstanding,* was the High Gear Bike Shop in Prescott, Arizona. Cindy Alwards, the proprietor, rescued me there from equipment issues that might have permanently injured my feet. At a time when I needed to be taken care of in order to go on, she was only too delighted to provide the attention I needed.

The best day's ride, at least the longest, was 120 miles. The day began in the northwest corner of New Mexico in the town of Clayton. We cut across the panhandle of Oklahoma and continued all the way to Hugoton, Kansas. The great distance was accomplished with the benefit of a rare and stiff tailwind that would not quit or even back off, all day long. We weren't even tired at the end of it!

The best ice cream was mint chocolate chip, although there were no disappointments with all the other good flavors. The best part of the ice cream experience was that we got to eat it as much and as often as we wanted. Sometimes we had it three or even four times a day. And to take the point a little further, we got to eat whatever else we wanted, too. The icing on the cake was that I came home 15 pounds lighter than when I'd left!

The best beer was... well, most of them were very good. An exception to that would be some of the selections that Bill made in an attempt to be frugal. There are some things for which frugality becomes a junior value. Beer is certainly one.

The best card game of the trip was euchre. For Kriss and me, euchre was a game that we were very familiar with, as it is the regional pastime of the Quad Cities area where we are originally from. Bill learned to play the game quickly and well though, as did the various SAG drivers. Parts of many evenings were spent at the euchre table, and so were a couple of rainy afternoons. It was always a way of spending enjoyable time together without any unnecessary physical exertion.

The best book I read on the trip was, *Lamb: the Gospel According to Biff, Christ's Childhood Pal*, by Christopher Moore. This bighearted, humorous and pithy version of the ancient story offers a very human expression of the divine central character, all through his buddy's eyes. Sometimes I would laugh until I cried and the guys wouldn't let up until I'd read them the passages out loud.

The best state for courteous drivers was Maryland. I have to say that, nationally, the standards are much lower for this than they ought to be. But Maryland rose far above the national standards. The state designated many of its highways as bike routes, and they invested in countless road signs that showed a picture of a stick person on a bicycle with the caption, *Share the Road*. The investment paid off; Maryland drivers were *by far* the best.

The most beautiful state was a toss-up for me between New Mexico and West Virginia. The incredible vistas and snow-covered passes of New Mexico's mountains contrasted by its endless deserts with cacti and myriad other forms of vegetation and wildlife were constantly awe inspiring. But then the lush and fertile rounded mountains of West Virginia with their winding streams and cascading forests were also inviting in a way that made me feel immediately appreciative and at home.

And the list goes on.

The racecar driver Mario Andretti spoke of excellence, "Desire is the key to motivation, but it is determination and commitment to an unrelenting pursuit of your goal - a commitment to excellence - that will enable you to attain the success you seek." We had a great deal of contact with excellence through the many bests that we enjoyed along the way. And while we couldn't make those things that were best happen, we were determined to recognize, appreciate and enjoy them. We were certainly committed to that!

When we curled up on our bunks inside Tiggie the night we finished the ride, we were feeling rather excellent altogether. We had begun our journey 46 days earlier with a dream and a goal. The pursuit of that goal had been unrelenting, just as had been the road that had constantly stretched out before us. As we drifted off to sleep just a few hundred feet from the water's edge, we were close enough to hear the waves of the ocean slapping up against the shore. There was no more road still waiting.

Epilogue II...

I woke up in my own bed at home in West Orange, New Jersey for the first time in 48 days on May 30th. I liked being home even though I didn't know what to think about the trip being over. I like my own bed and we have one of the best showers at our house that I've ever used anywhere. I liked waking up with Judy and having breakfast together at our own table.

And while Bill and I were at home in West Orange, Kriss was not. Because he too wanted to be at home and because he is an incredible introvert, he opted to skip out on the day's very social agenda. After making arrangements to have his bike shipped to back to Iowa, we dropped him off at Penn Station so he could catch a train out of Newark early that morning.

It was Saturday and Sabine von Aulock, our consummate church woman and planner extraordinaire, had made some big plans to welcome Bill and I back home. Sabine never does things in a small way! With Rickey behind the wheel and Judy at shotgun, Tiggie made its last run as our SAG wagon for one more short ride. Following close behind, Bill and I rode our bikes a few blocks to Eagle Rock Nature Reservation. We got there at about 11 o'clock. There were several dozen people already there awaiting our arrival. Many of them had come on their own bicycles, and some by car.

I knew most of the people at the gathering. There were lots of folks from my congregation including much of our leadership and the Mayor of Montclair. But there were also a few people who I'd never met before, who had come along because they'd heard about our trip. Some of them had even followed us along the way on Bill's Blog.

They were all gathered near the parking lot, next to a high cliff overlooking the Passaic and Hudson River valleys, a place with a phenomenal view of New York City. As we approached, a roar of welcome erupted. It was not your everyday sort of experience. I've been welcomed heartily by groups of people before, but never in such Lindbergh-ian style.

I found myself thinking two things as I rode into the waiting crowd. First, I was really glad Kriss had decided to skip this experience. It was not the sort of thing he would abide easily. The sudden shift from mile after mile of considerable solitude to finding himself thrust into any kind of limelight might have been fatal, certainly unbearable. I suspected he was very happy at that same moment, sitting on his westbound Amtrak train, reading a book and occasionally looking out the window, musing over the transition from one adventure to the next.

The other thing that occurred to me was that... I *was* there. I did have to respond! Eagle Rock was filled with joyful well-wishers, with all kinds of enthusiasm, and I needed to respond. I had to think about it for all of about 10 seconds before my natural responses kicked in. As we rode into this crowd of people that I hadn't seen in nearly two months, I was beaming, and waving and throwing kisses to everyone left and right.

How wonderful to be greeted by these folks who had supported us from a distance all the way across the country on our journey. The trip really was much bigger than any of the three of us. It was much bigger than the three of us put together. It had been about Toni's Kitchen, and about the larger community. It'd been about my congregation and their gift to me of this sabbatical. Now everyone was there to celebrate and that sure felt like the right thing to me.

After visiting on the mountaintop for a while, it was time to ride down into Montclair and to Toni's Kitchen. Everyone who was there with a bike joined the ride as we rode down the face of the mountain, along the road that snaked its way through the reservation and released us at the bottom into town. The local paper was there and an action photo was taken to record the moment. It would be printed on the front page of the following week's edition.

We rode into St. Luke's Church parking lot, just outside of the Toni's Kitchen door. There, the whole celebration started all over again. This time Mary Ann Renn, Executive Director of TK's, led it and the crowd was made up of the many wonderful volunteers and guests who'd all followed our progress across the country online. Again, the celebration was very contagious.

We all had lunch at TK's and there were a few speeches. A large jar filled mostly with coins but also a few bills that had been collected among the guests at Toni's Kitchen was a presented to me so that it could be added to the other contributions that had been made. It was a very touching experience, one filled with considerable satisfaction and appreciation for all of the people involved in Toni's Kitchen.

Then we were back on our bikes again. This time we rode the few blocks over to the Unitarian Universalist Congregation, where the whole thing repeated itself yet another time with a whole new crowd from my congregation. As that party began to wind down a couple of hours later, there was a young man, Gary, in his early 20's, who I've known most of his life. He'd been waiting behind the crowd, so he and I could talk.

Gary told me that he'd be leaving the next day himself, for a cross-country bicycle trip. There were a few things he wanted to ask me about. Gary and I spent the next three hours or so taking tires apart and putting them back together, going over tool lists and clothing inventories. We talked about the challenges that lay ahead for him.

"Do you think I'm crazy for doing this, Charlie?" He asked. "Do you think I can do it?"

"Gary," I said, "I don't know if you can do it or not. I suspect that if I can do this, nearly anyone who can ride a bike could do it. I don't know if you can make it all the way across the country or not, but I don't even think that that's what matters. What matters is that there is an adventure in front of you, and it's calling your name. I trust that you'll be okay, and that you'll do the things that you need to do. I know that you will discover parts of the world that otherwise you would have missed. And I know that you'll discover parts of yourself that otherwise you couldn't possibly find. I believe in you, Gary. Have a great ride." And, I'm happy to say, he did...

For weeks after we got back, whenever I'd see anyone whom I hadn't seen since returning, they'd always ask, "So how was that bike ride of yours?"

It took a while, but my typical answer began to take a shape. "Well," I'd say, "it was wonderful and it was terrible. It was beautiful and it was ugly. It was the most wonderful thing I've ever done, and it was one of the most difficult things I've ever done. It was the best and it was the worst. And altogether... it was quite exquisite." It really had been all of those things individually. The sum of those many parts though... was truly magnificent.

The eminent poet, T.S. Eliot, wrote:
"What we call a beginning is often the end
and to make an end is to make a beginning.
The end is where we start from.

We shall not cease from exploration
and the end of all our exploring
will be to arrive where we started
and know the place for the first time."

Who knows where a journey like this might end? Or if it ever will?

The metaphors and lessons in this book are a part of an *adventure journey,* which is a metaphor for life itself. The stories are intended to share my experiences from the road, but more, they are intended to encourage you, the reader, (or listener) to find your way into the lessons of your own journeys. In our fast-paced, spiritually scattered world, we can all use whatever help we might find to encourage and enable us to take the time for tuning into our own lives – so that we might find more joy, so that we might find and make greater meaning in them. My hope is that, "Moving on..." has provided you with such an opportunity. Thanks for coming along. Moving on...

ACKNOWLEDGMENTS

I suspect that nothing of note occurs in a vacuum. Instead, meaningful projects come out of an environment that is teeming with gracious participants. *Moving On*, has had the benefit of such an environment and so I have many to thank:

Ω   The teachers who have helped to shape my life and my skills: Betty Nelson Kopp, Alan Egly, Merrilea Trawin and Robert Karnan;

Ω   Those who served as both cheerleaders and literary guides for this work: Elizabeth Stone, John Monteleone, Michael Nolan and Rosemary Bray McNatt;

Ω   Those who were faced with the daunting task of proofreading this material: Judy Ortman and the indefatigable Jaclyn Puleo;

Ω   Bill Slezak for his stunning cover photo;

Ω   Those back home who made it possible for a bike ride to become a community event: The Unitarian Universalist Congregation at Montclair provided me with sabbatical leave and loving support, the quintessential arrangements person, Sabine von Aulock, single-handedly planned and executed all of the fundraising efforts and events, Mary Ann Renn and all the folks at Toni's Kitchen gave me loving support and lots of prayers;

Ω   The greatest riding team imaginable, who not only helped me become a better rider but a more attentive person: Bill Slezak and Kriss Wells, as well as our Supply and Gear masters Dennis Barnum, Martha Easter-Wells, Jay Bowman, Rickey Slezak and Judy Ortman;

Ω   And finally, Judy Ortman, without whose love, understanding, support and encouragement, I would likely have never done any of this.

ABOUT THE AUTHOR

Born in Kankakee, Illinois in 1950, Charles Ortman was raised mostly in Rock Island, IL.. He attended Catholic primary and secondary schools, where he received an excellent education and not too much harm to his psyche. His undergraduate work, which began at the height of the Vietnam War, spanned a period, off and on, of some seventeen years. The non-school years were spent working as a Conscientious Objector and as a non-degreed social worker, in locations from inner-city Chicago to the rural hills of northwestern Illinois.

Those years also included travel in the United States and Europe as an itinerant musician. He recorded an album of original songs in 1987, "New Moon," on Desert Rose Music. He graduated with honors from Western Illinois University in 1985. Three years later he began working on a Master of Divinity degree at Meadville/Lombard Seminary, affiliated with The University of Chicago. He graduated and was ordained to the Unitarian Universalist ministry in 1992. Since then he has served congregations in Burlington, IA, Fitchburg, MA, and has been with the UU Congregation in Montclair, NJ for the past 17 years. Writing has been a passionate activity – including both love and hate – for all of these years.

Charles married Judy Blustein in 1978. Together, they are the exceedingly proud parents of three incredible human beings, Will, Laura and Shana, each accomplished in their own right. He says that, "No single event has so profoundly changed my life as the moment I first became a father. Except of course all of the moments that have come since."

Made in the USA
Charleston, SC
19 September 2013